BIBLE TREASURES

BOOKS BY IVOR POWELL —

Bible Highways
   Studies and Illustrations in "Highways" Through the Bible

Bible Treasures
   Treasures of Truest Worth From the World's Richest Storehouse

Bible Pinnacles
   Character Sketches, Pivotal Incidents, Miracles and Parables

Bible Windows
   Anecdotes and Stories Suitable for Sermon Illustrations

Bible Cameos
   Biographies From the Oldest and Most Up-to-Date Book, Graphically Portrayed

BIBLE TREASURES

IVOR POWELL

With a Foreword by Dr. Lionel B. Fletcher

ZONDERVAN PUBLISHING HOUSE
GRAND RAPIDS, MICHIGAN

This American edition is published by special
arrangement with the British publisher,
Marshall, Morgan & Scott, Ltd., of London.
No part to be reproduced without permission.

First Published.......1953
American Edition.....1960

Printed in the United States of America

FOREWORD

As the last of the evangelists of my generation who travelled through the Empire seeking men for Christ, it is a glad experience to write a Foreword to Ivor Powell's new book, *Bible Treasures,* as he is a well-known Empire evangelist of this new generation. I pray that he may be used mightily to win thousands for Christ and His Church.

Bible Treasures! Very few people know how great are the treasures awaiting discovery in the old Book which the Holy Spirit inspired men to write. Men and women go mad with excitement, and risk all their possessions in the quest for earthly treasures. This I very well know, for every old " gold diggings " in Australia has a story of " a lost reef " of gold, and constantly men dream of the time when its discovery will lead to their boundless wealth.

As a youth of 18, I sat one morning under an old cow endeavouring to fill a bucket with milk. I was also dreaming of " the lost reef " of gold when I heard the thunder of galloping horses and the yells of excited people. Our house was a mile or more from the nearest neighbour, so I was startled, and ran to find out what was happening. I saw about a score of excited people who, as they rode upon all kinds of horses, waved axes, shovels, and other implements, and as they vanished into the bush, cried out, " The lost reef's found. The lost reef's found." I would have left all in order to follow the mad mob, had not the calm voice of my brother said, " You had better get on with the milking, and then attend to the other jobs." I spluttered, " But they have found the lost reef; we will lose the opportunity of making a fortune." He smiled and told me to get on with my work, and allow others to ascertain whether or not the report were true.

The lost reef is still lost, for although some men did get a little gold from the new diggings, others lost more than was ever discovered there. I know that to my cost, for I lost all my savings when I paid another enthusiastic youth to dig in my stead. He found nothing, and I had to supply both his food and his wages!

Then and in later years I saw the recklessness of people who were seized with "gold fever"—the passion for earthly treasure. Yet these same seekers, for a few shillings, could purchase *The Book* which Ivor Powell opens to us in these pages. The Scriptures represent the greatest gold reef in the world, which God Himself has given to us. Alas, these "lost treasures," in spite of the fact that they offer eternal riches, are lost, because most people do not give the time and effort to seek for them.

I am glad and thankful that this evangelist is a gifted writer, and that in addition to his preaching he has compiled for his readers a store of Bible Treasures, which will yield to all who accept them, riches for evermore.

LIONEL B. FLETCHER.

CONTENTS

	Page
FOREWORD by Lionel B. Fletcher	v
INTRODUCTION	x
MAN . . . and evolution in reverse	1
ENOCH . . . and the baby which changed his life	3
ABRAM . . . and his excellent eye-exercises	5
ABRAHAM . . . and a bunch of rogues	7
LOT'S WIFE . . . who was buried alive	9
JOSEPH . . . whose funeral lasted 450 years	11
MOSES . . . who tried to get out of a job	13
MOSES . . . who supplied Christ with a sermon illustration	15
MOSES . . . who preached about an eagle	17
JOSHUA . . . and his prophetic symbolism	19
THE FIVE KINGS . . . who were in a hole	21
DAGON . . . who reappears in other temples	23
DAVID . . . and his habit of slaying giants	25
SAUL . . . who seemed to be hypnotized	27
BARZILLAI . . . who went home to wait for God	29
JOAB . . . who lacked staying power	31
OBADIAH . . . whose widow complained	33
ELISHA . . . and the slaughter of the innocents	35
JABEZ . . . the giant among dwarfs	37
JEHOSHAPHAT . . . who was known by his prayer	39
JEHOIADA AND JOASH . . . or the tale of two funerals	41
UZZIAH . . . and a family in decline	43
THE BIRDS . . . which were wiser than men	45
THE GARDENER . . . who neglected his weeding	47
FOUR MIDGETS . . . and their secret of strength	49
MR. INSIGNIFICANCE . . . who should have been knighted	51
THE APOTHECARY . . . who had flies in his ointment	53
THE CHURCH . . . as she ought to be	55
ISAIAH . . . who loved drawing water out of wells	57
ISAIAH . . . who saw God's love in disguise	59
ISAIAH . . . and his broken pen	61
ISAIAH . . . the man with the telescopic sight	63
EZEKIEL . . . and his sermon about three great men	65

	Page
HAGGAI ... the prophet with a punch	67
ZECHARIAH ... and his comprehensive picture of the Gospel	69
CHRIST ... and His gracious invitation	71
THE HOLY SPIRIT ... and the unpardonable sin ...	73
THE GOLD DIGGER ... and the way he staked his claim	75
THE FUNERAL OF JOHN ... and its glorious sequel ...	77
THE SILENCE OF CHRIST ... which preached to a world	79
CHRIST ... and the eternal bulldozer	81
THE GREAT WEDDING ... and the people who came late	83
CHRIST ... and the tale of two cities	85
CHRIST ... and a unique sense of values ...	87
FIVE HEADS ... with but a single thought	89
SIMON THE LEPER ... who remembered to be grateful	91
PETER ... who had the shock of his life ...	93
THE MAN ... whose right hand was withered ...	95
CHRIST ... and the requirements of the new life ...	97
CHRIST ... and His commentary on preaching ...	99
THE LAWYER AND THE RULER ... who asked the same question	101
THE HOUSE OF MERCY ... on the Jericho road ...	103
CHRIST ... who prayed for Peter	105
CHRIST ... and the breaking of the bread ...	107
CHRIST ... and three steps to a golden throne ...	109
ANDREW ... the patron saint of all personal workers	111
THE UNIQUE CHRIST ... and His glorious incomparability	113
THE APOSTLES ... and the life more abundant ...	115
THE GOOD SHEPHERD ... and a wonderful promise	117
CHRIST ... and three out-of-season fruits	119
CHRIST ... and His tantalizing inconsistency ...	121
TWO MEN ... who triumphed in the end	123
PETER ... who was told to mind his own business	125
THE CHURCH ... and the first Seventh Day Adventists	127
PAUL AND BARNABAS ... whom we invite to a debate	129
PAUL ... who left the mainspring out of his watch	131
PAUL ... who could be as stubborn as a mule ...	133
PAUL ... who proved it's an ill wind that blows no good	135

	Page
PAUL ... and the greatness of God's salvation ...	137
PAUL ... and the ministry of women	139
PAUL ... and his advice about walking	141
PAUL ... who wrote the shortest life-story of Christ	143
THE PRECIOUS BLOOD OF CHRIST ... the master-key	145
PAUL ... who believed in the return of his Lord ...	147
ONESIPHORUS ... who loved to visit a prison ...	149
PAUL ... who met a prodigal son	151
CHRIST ... and the nastiest taste in the world ...	153
THE ROYAL HIGHWAY ... or milestones on the road to heaven	155
GOD'S ART GALLERY ... and three of its wonderful pictures	157
JOHN ... and his yardstick of truth	159
THE CHURCH AT PERGAMOS ... and the little white stone	161
THE LAMB ... the alpha and omega of God's revelation	163
ALPHABETICAL INDEX	165
COMPREHENSIVE INDEX	167

INTRODUCTION BY THE AUTHOR

I am grateful to God and to an appreciative public for the magnificent way in which the two previous volumes in this series, *Bible Cameos* and *Bible Pinnacles,* have been received. Little did I realize when I wrote the first of these, that it would lead to others of its type. Day after day, however, ministers and laymen expressed their gratitude, and asked if I had other books of the same kind. Their requests stimulated my own interest, and volume two was written. I now send forth the third volume, with the sincere hope that many young ministers may find treasure untold within its pages. However, I would stress again that these books are not systematic commentaries. I have tried, not to supply a new commentary, but rather to assist preachers and teachers in the art of formulating, dividing, and presenting the treasures found in Holy Scripture. The readers of these books will undoubtedly find expositions, as these are the natural corollary of any endeavour to handle Bible truths. I remind students that the best way to find treasure here, is first of all to read the Scripture passage to be considered. Let the Word of God be fresh in your mind before you study my comments. I do not recommend the practice of reading four or five of these chapters before going to bed. Read first the Bible, and then consider my remarks. In this way treasure may be discovered.

I am deeply grateful to Dr. Lionel Fletcher for his kindness in writing the Foreword to this new book. Dr. Fletcher was a minister in Cardiff, South Wales, when I was a small boy. His powerful ministry, and his crowded church, left indelible impressions upon my young life. During my long period of crusading in South Africa, I usually finished campaigns with a testimony meeting in which people were given the opportunity to tell where and when they were won for Christ. My joy was boundless when, time after time, I heard fine men and women say, " I was won for Christ in Lionel Fletcher's meetings." Some of these people had become valiant workers for Christ, and the fragrant winsomeness and the undeniable power of their ministry reached entire communities. Lionel Fletcher's work cannot die ; he can never be forgotten, for his name is written on multitudes of hearts. I am happy to acknowledge his gracious Foreword, and as he has expressed, I trust my readers will find treasure in this and the other volumes of the Bible series.

IVOR POWELL.

MAN... and evolution in reverse
(GENESIS 4 : 16-26)

"And Cain went out from the presence of the Lord," and abject despair reigned in his heart. He had cried to God, "My punishment is greater than I can bear. Behold, thou hast driven me out this day from the face of the earth . . . and it shall come to pass, that every one that findeth me shall slay me." He had discovered that the way of transgressors is hard; that the world can be a very lonely place. Yet Cain was a great fighter, and as time healed the wound in his pride he became exceedingly resourceful.

Astounding Growth

What is this? A city! Cain, you wonderful fellow! It seems impossible that you could have performed such a miracle. Perhaps your city would not compare with the modern monstrosities which sprawl over the face of the earth; but at least, with your own hands, and without much assistance, you foresaw an increasing need, and with bricks baked hard in the sunshine, you solved your housing problems. And your cattle, too! What wonderful herds you possessed; and even your children profited from your example, for "Adah bare Jabal: he was the father of such as dwell in tents, and of such as have cattle." When necessity drove your children far from their permanent homes, they made tents and became nomads. Cain, your people were amazing! When they sat in the cool of those ancient nights and looked at the stars, the music of the eternal demanded expression. "And Jabal's brother's name was Jubal: he was the father of all such as handle the harp or organ." Yes, Cain, your children were the first musicians in the world, and their harps thrilled the ancients. "And Zillah, she also bare Tubal-Cain, an instructor of every artificer in brass and iron." He produced ploughs, tools, building materials; he was the father of the modern foundries, the vast steel works, and the chimneys belching forth clouds of blackness. Cain, when all seemed lost, you fought back well. You were a wonderful fellow.

Another Grave

"And Lamech said unto his wives, Adah and Zillah . . . I have slain a man to my wounding, and a young man to my hurt. If Cain shall be avenged sevenfold, truly Lamech seventy and sevenfold." What a shame that the growth of man's soul did not keep pace with his advancing civilization. He overcame the difficulties of survival; he mastered some of the great secrets of the earth: yet in spite of all his remarkable achievements, he failed to conquer himself. He created a wonderful environment in which to spend his days, yet he never tamed the tiger in his own heart. A difference of opinion; smouldering passions; vehement opposition; a sudden blow, and once again tragedy had darkened God's world. A young man lay dead, and the corpse seemed strangely out of place amid the products of civilization. Clever man had to pause awhile to dig another grave. There were no tears of penitence, but just a bullying claim for absolution from punishment. He was entitled to eleven times more protection than that afforded to his father, because, after all, his capabilities made him of greater value to the world. He was a great man. He could maintain cities, increase his flocks, train musicians, create foundries. He was indispensable—he was like God.

Amazing Grace

It was significant that God waited to give man his chance. The grace of God only moved to the rescue of a fallen race when foolish sinners had demonstrated their depravity. "And Adam knew his wife again; and she bare a son, and called his name Seth: For God, said she, hath appointed me another seed instead of Abel, whom Cain slew. And to Seth, to him also there was born a son; and he called his name Enos: *then began men to call on the name of the Lord.*" Man's failure has ever been a challenge to the resources of God. His grace always supplies the remedy when sinful man is bankrupt. Through Seth came the godly line of descendants in whose hearts prayer was born. These people recognized that advancing civilization had its rightful place in the world, and yet at the same time it could not satisfy the inherent requirements of human hearts. They needed God. In all probability they sought remote corners, and when the burdens of life became intolerably heavy, they knelt to pray. Thus they discovered spiritual gold reefs in the desolate wilderness of human failure. They prayed, and God heard them.

The ancient story shows evolution in reverse. A man increases his stature when he learns to kneel.

ENOCH... and the baby which changed his life
(Genesis 5: 21-24)

A baby is a mighty atom; the outstanding example of dynamic helplessness. Its smiling eyes can remove mountains; its gurgles of merriment can delight an empire, and produce chuckles of delight in ancients who have long since forgotten the days of their youth. Its tiny fingers, unable to hold the lightest article, can effectively grasp the hearts of all who watch it; the small feet, unable as yet to take one step, can ruthlessly march into the inner precincts of any heart; and the eyes which as yet cannot recognize a mother, can captivate and enthral a world. Its wrath can take the sunshine from a home. Its insistent cries for attention can bring kings and queens running to its side. Its likes and dislikes can govern families. His Lordship the Baby is the master of ceremonies in every abode. It has been thus from the beginning of time. One of the greatest men of the ancient world owed everything to the coming of his baby. When he looked into the innocent face of a helpless child, his entire outlook was changed, and he was never the same again.

How Thrilling the Methods of God

"And Enoch lived sixty and five years, and begat Methuselah: And Enoch walked with God *after he begat Methuselah* three hundred years, and begat sons and daughters." It is significant that the beginning of Enoch's walking with God dates from the birth of his first child. The sacred record is content to say that Enoch merely lived for the first sixty-five years of his sojourn on earth. He was like any other man. He fulfilled the normal functions and requirements of existence. He lived as a man among men. Then suddenly everything was changed. The expected baby arrived, and from that moment the father was amazingly transformed. The glad event transported him to heights of joy hitherto unknown; and when the unprecedented ecstasy had passed, the proud father was left with a consuming desire to keep in step with God. The Almighty had sent this inestimable gift, and gratitude could only be expressed in holy conduct. How strange are the ways of God! A baby accomplished in one moment what sixty-five years of experience had failed to do.

How Transcendent the Man of God

The child was named Methuselah. Many and varied interpretations of the meaning of this strange name have been given. Certain scholars have declared that it means

"Man of the dart or javelin." Yet another startling suggestion is that the name Methuselah means, "It shall not come till he die" (Lange's Commentary). Jude, in the 14th verse of his short epistle, says that Enoch the seventh from Adam was a prophet who foresaw an outpouring of judgment upon sinful people. Thus it would appear that in naming his child, the father indicated that a great spiritual revelation had been linked with the birth of his baby. It is even more startling to notice that the prediction was fulfilled. Methuselah was destined to become famous, for he lived longer than any other person. He reached the age of nine hundred and sixty-nine years; but in the year of his death, the great flood devastated the earth. This awesome truth was clearly seen by Enoch long before it happened, and although the name Methuselah had never been given to a child, no other name could possibly meet the requirements of the new arrival. Whenever the proud father nursed his son, he remembered his great revelation, and calmly walked with his Lord.

How Tremendous the Mercy of God

"And all the days of Enoch were three hundred sixty and five years: And Enoch walked with God: and he was not; for God took him." Amid the increasing corruption of earth, this saint was out of place, and ultimately God translated him to higher and nobler society. But Methuselah lived on and on. Possibly some men thought he would never die; that he had discovered the secret of perennial youth. Yet we know now that the length of the patriarch's life was an indication of the overwhelming mercy of God. "It shall not come till he die." The Homecall of the aged man would coincide with the closure of God's offer of mercy to a guilty world. Thus he was allowed to linger. When other people were taken away, he remained; and every day of his long life proved to be another opportunity for men to repent. Alas, the spiritual state of the people constantly deteriorated, and finally the Lord repented that He had ever made man. During that year Methuselah died, and his decease was followed by outpoured judgment. Enoch recognized all this when his son was born. His life was changed by innocent helplessness—a baby boy.

ABRAM ... and his excellent eye-exercises
(Genesis 13: 7–18)

"And Abram went up out of Egypt" (13:1), and probably he was very glad to go. The land of the Pharaohs had been an unpleasant place for the man who had been called to Canaan. His sense of the divine Presence had been lost, and every day registered increasing misery. He had long since regretted the decision to leave Bethel's altar, and wished he could forget the moment when his covetous eyes desired the attractions of Egypt. At last his restless spirit had found relief, and he returned "to the altar which he had made at the beginning" (v. 4). Slowly he journeyed through the country, and a prayer of thanksgiving arose from his lips when the familiar landmarks came into view. The vision of the altar meant more than possession of a mighty palace.

Abram's Increasing Wisdom

"And there was a strife between the herdmen of Abram's cattle and the herdmen of Lot's cattle: and the Canaanite and the Perizzite dwelled then in the land. And Abram said unto Lot, Let there be no strife, I pray thee, between me and thee, and between my herdmen and thy herdmen; for we be brethren. Is not the whole land before thee?" (vv. 7-9). The wise old man had learned to hate discord. It was not only a very bad example to the watching Canaanites, it was ruinous to his own happiness. "Lot, you may have the rich pasture lands; you may journey in any direction acceptable to you. You may choose anything; but do not spoil my fellowship with God and man." The saint looked toward Egypt, and shuddered; he looked around in every direction, and sighed; he looked to the sky, and smiled. Nothing mattered any more but to walk with God. "Lot, my boy, the whole land is before you. Yours is the choice to go whithersoever you desire. Take the land; take the well-watered places; take it all, only leave me at peace with God."

Abram's Incessant Watchfulness

"And Lot lifted up his eyes and beheld the plain of Jordan, that it was well watered everywhere.... Then Lot chose him all the plain of Jordan; and Lot journeyed *east*; and they separated themselves the one from the other" (vv. 10, 11). And perhaps old uncle Abram sighed as the boy went away. Regret and relief mingled in his fatherly heart. He was sad for the boy's sake, but profoundly glad for his own. His nephew had probably said, "You don't mind, Uncle Abram, if I take the rich and luscious pasture lands in the valley to the east? It seems a mean thing to leave an old man with the hills and stony ground; but I would like to live near the cities, to trade with the people of Sodom, and to exploit these far-reaching meadows. I am sure you will be rewarded even if you do lose these eastern pastures. You don't mind, do you? No, I thought not; you were always such a wonderful uncle to me." When Abram turned his back on the inviting district of Sodom, his soul sang. What did it matter that he had lost fertile lands and a vast opportunity for increasing wealth? He was happy; he was at peace; he walked with the Highest: all was well. He looked again at the plains of Jordan and said, in so many words, "What shall it profit a man if he gain the whole world and lose his soul?" He looked at the difficult terrain ahead, and said, "If God be for us, who can be against us?" He looked at the skies, and a voice whispered, "Be not afraid, for I am with thee whithersoever thou goest." And as the glory of God filled his soul, his eyes became stars.

Abram's Inspired Worship

"And the Lord said unto Abram, after that Lot was separated from him, Lift up now thine eyes, and look from the place where thou art, northward, and southward, and *eastward,* and westward: For *all* the land which thou seest, to thee will I give it" (v. 14). "But, Lord, all the land to the east now belongs to Lot." And God answered, "To thee will I give it, and to thy seed for ever." Lot, in grasping for material gain, loses it; your renunciation of it brings it within your reach. Abram, lift up your eyes and see all the land before you. It is yours; for those eyes see most, which first look to the skies. "Arise, walk through the land in the length of it and in the breadth of it; for I will give it unto thee. Then Abram removed his tent and came and dwelt in the plain of Mamre, which is in Hebron, and built there an altar unto the Lord." Daily he journeyed among the hills where Sodom's smoke had little chance of getting into his eyes. He had excellent vision—he even saw Christ's day, and was glad.

ABRAHAM ... and a bunch of rogues
(GENESIS 18: 27)

Self-esteem is rarely found in the heart of a true man of God, for the more virtuous a saint becomes, the less satisfied he will be with himself. Increasing love for God means increasing hatred of the self-life. The Bible has many examples of this fact.

Abraham. " I am but dust and ashes "—Genesis 18:27.

Abraham was the friend of God, and the greatest character in the ancient world. Divine secrets were shared with the illustrious patriarch, and in a sense unknown by ordinary men, he walked with God. Yet Abraham despised himself, and became increasingly conscious of his shortcomings. He considered himself unworthy to commune with God, and said he was dust and ashes.

Job. " Behold, I am vile "—Job 40:4.

We are left in no doubt as to the true greatness of this man. It is recorded that the Lord said of him " ... there is none like him in the earth, a perfect and an upright man, one that feareth God, and escheweth evil " (Job 1:8). When Job's friends declared him to be a hypocrite; that secret sin had brought about his misfortunes, he maintained that his heart was clean before God. Yet when he came face to face with his Maker, he whispered, " I am vile."

David. " Behold, I was shapen in iniquity "—Psalm 51:5.

The sweet psalmist of Israel was a man after God's own heart, and although certain indiscretions marred his fine record of devotion, his integrity and true consecration were always beyond question. Yet this great man sadly shook his head and denied his own virtue. Psalm 51 is a heart-throb in which we hear tears of anguish, cries of disappointment, and the moan of a man who feels that he is a complete failure.

Ezra. " I blush to lift up my face "—Ezra 9:6.

Ezra was one of the greatest men of his day. He held an honourable place among the spiritual aristocracy of the nation. His courageous example at a time when Israel needed spiritual leadership, lifted the nation to new heights of achievement. He and Nehemiah were the greatest men of that generation; yet Ezra's confession claimed for him a place in Rogues' Gallery. He said, "O my God, I am ashamed and blush to lift up my face."

Isaiah. "I am undone . . . I am a man of unclean lips"—Isaiah 6:5.

Isaiah was one of the major prophets, who gave counsel and guidance to a stumbling nation, and at the same time provided unerring information concerning the coming of the Messiah. He was a friend of the king, a father to the nation, and a trusted servant of the Most High; yet of himself he had nothing good to say.

Simon Peter. "I am a sinful man"—Luke 5:8

There is something delightfully human about Simon Peter, for at all times he was unquestionably honest. Sometimes strong emotions and fierce temptations upset his equilibrium; but within minutes, the real man appeared again. He was a great man, an excellent preacher, and a brother beloved. Yet all who read the New Testament realize how very much Peter abhorred himself.

The Centurion. "I am not worthy"—Luke 7:6.

This Gentile soldier won a place among the great immortals, for his spiritual perception enabled Christ to say, "I have not found so great faith, no, not in Israel." Although he was an officer in Caesar's army, and occupied a position of importance, he felt that his home was unworthy of a visit from the Carpenter of Nazareth.

Paul. "I am the chief of sinners"—1 Timothy 1:15.

Paul was undoubtedly the greatest of all Christian missionaries. He was the first to look beyond the narrow bounds of Israel's horizons, and with determination of purpose to penetrate into the unknown. His indomitable spirit and untiring energy took the Gospel to millions of heathen, and with God's help he established the Christian Church. Yet Paul claimed to be the greatest sinner in the world.

God has strange ways of estimating the greatness of men. Sometimes the first are last, and the last first. Those who are great in their own estimation are far from the will of God, while others who are overwhelmed by a sense of unworthiness are ready for the Master's use. A bunch of rogues? No: some of God's great gentlemen!

LOT'S WIFE ... who was buried alive
(Genesis 19: 26)

> A Bible character without a name,
> Who never to corruption came:
> Who died a death none ever died before,
> Whose shroud forms part of every household store.

Lot's wife, of course! But based as it is upon old-fashioned beliefs, this quaint verse is untrue. Archæological and geological findings have shed new light upon the ancient account, and modern critics have been confounded. We know now that the cities of the plain perished in flames, just as the Bible describes. The historical record is absolutely true.

A Sure Word

"Then the Lord rained upon Sodom and upon Gomorrah brimstone and fire from the Lord out of heaven ; and he overthrew those cities, and all the plain, and all the inhabitants of the cities, and that which grew upon the ground" (Gen. 19: 24, 25). Modern discoveries have revealed that the ancient cities were built over an oil field, and that this has been burnt out. Geologists have also discovered faults in the strata of the earth, on either side of what was once the cities of the plain. To complete the picture, a layer of rock salt can be seen throughout the entire district. In some strange way the salt deposits of the earth were flung into the air, finally to fall in tremendous quantities over the entire neighbourhood. Thus the ancient scene can be reconstructed. At the time when Lot entered his city of refuge, an earthquake rocked the district, and the cities within the limits of the faults slipped into the earth. The terrific pressure thus brought to bear upon the underlying oil, forced millions of gallons high into the air, where it became ignited, to fall in burning masses upon the doomed habitations. Lifted by irresistible forces, vast quantities of disintegrating rock salt were flung upward, to fall later as a gigantic snow-storm. Overtaken by this unprecedented disaster, Lot's wife was instantly buried and suffocated. She became the inside of a pillar of salt, and perished within a short distance of her husband's refuge.

A Stupid Woman

"And it came to pass, when the angels had brought them forth abroad, that one said, Escape for thy life ; *look not behind thee,* neither stay thou in all the plain ; escape to the mountain, lest thou be consumed" (v. 17). Releasing his hold upon the hand of Lot's wife, the angel sent her hurrying to safety. If she had ever recognized the urgency of her need, she ignored it, and slowly decreasing her speed, she paused to look back at the place she had left for ever. Who was she? In all probability Lot had lived in Sodom for twenty years. His children had been born and brought up within the environs of that wicked city. It is truly significant that, while his sons stayed behind with their brothers-in-law (v. 12), Lot's two daughters were willing to leave their husbands in order to accompany their father. The boys belonged to the "younger set," and loved the attractions of Sodom. In her scramble for safety, the mother remembered the things she had left behind. She had heard and partially believed the angels' message, but obedience demanded a degree of sacrifice she seemed unwilling to give. While her husband frantically rushed for safety, she lingered and died within sight of the open gates. The earth trembled; the atmosphere was set alight, and her terrified screams were suddenly stifled.

A Serious Warning

When the Lord Jesus was asked for signs of His return, He said, "Likewise also as it was in the days of Lot; they did eat, they drank, they bought, they sold, they planted, they builded; but the same day that Lot went out of Sodom, it rained fire and brimstone from heaven, and destroyed them all. Even thus shall it be in the day when the Son of man shall be revealed. In that day, he which shall be upon the housetop, and his stuff in the house, let him not come down to take it away: and he that is in the field, let him likewise not return back. *Remember Lot's wife*" (Luke 17:28-32). This suggests that she hesitated because she suddenly remembered possessions left behind in her home. Thus Christ taught that nothing should ever be allowed to interfere with our readiness to meet the returning Lord. If we place our hand to the plough, and then look back, we advertise our unfitness for a place in His eternal kingdom. Most people erect monuments with their hands: Lot's wife erected hers with her feet.

JOSEPH . . . whose funeral lasted 450 years
(GENESIS 50: 25)

Joseph died 450 years before he was finally buried. His funeral procession was the longest in history—it extended through four centuries. As friends and descendants followed the bier, it became necessary to change the bearers many times, for the faithful men who served in this capacity aged and died. It is not too much to say that before the bones of Joseph were laid to rest, thousands of Israelites passed away. As the dignified procession proceeded, onlooking nations wondered why ceremonial should be so observed. They probably found it difficult to understand why the strange Israelites refused to dig a grave immediately. Solemn vows dictated Israel's actions, for their fathers had told them how "Joseph took an oath of the children of Israel, saying, God will surely visit you, and ye shall carry up my bones from hence."

The Bones of Remembrance

"So Joseph died, being an hundred and ten years old: and they embalmed him, and he was put in a coffin in Egypt" (v. 26). Thus ended the earthly career of one of God's greatest servants. His foresight and unsullied purity had gained an abiding place in the affections of his brethren; they never forgot how he had saved them during the distressing famine which devastated Egypt. Knowing that God would restore Israel to their own land, the patriarch requested that his mortal remains should accompany the redeemed people; that on no account should his bones be left in an alien land. When he died, his body was carefully embalmed and placed in a coffin; but it was never buried. Probably it was given an honoured resting place, and this became a shrine. Whenever visitors stood silently before the sacred casket, they remembered gratefully the one who had brought their salvation, and were constantly reminded of their increasing debt of gratitude.

The Bones of Responsibility

The years passed by, and ultimately the faith of Joseph was vindicated. "And it came to pass, when Pharaoh had let the people go . . . Moses took the bones of Joseph with him: for he had straitly sworn the children of Israel, saying, God will surely visit you; and ye shall carry up my bones away hence with you" (Exod. 13:17-19). Thus did Moses lead the nation out of the land of bondage; but even he did not realize the journey to Canaan would last forty years. The sacred remains of their beloved ancestor were not finally buried until Israel possessed the promised land. When the invasion of Canaan had been brought satisfactorily to a conclusion, the people assembled for the strangest and most delayed funeral service ever known. "And the bones of Joseph, which the children of Israel brought up out of Egypt, buried they in Shechem, in a parcel of ground which Jacob bought of the sons of Hamor the father of Shechem for a hundred pieces of silver: and it became the inheritance of the children of Joseph" (Josh. 24:32). During the entire period no treasure was afforded greater protection than that given to the sacred bones of their ancient saviour. Thus the Egyptian coffin accompanied them everywhere, and the very fact that Israel revered its contents guaranteed that ultimately God would bring His people to their land of rest.

The Bones of Resemblance

It would be easy for us to imagine Moses saying, "We must do this till He come." When we remember how that ancient funeral procession extended through the years; when we consider the affectionate devotion with which the coffin was carried, we think of Another who made a similar request. Many years of arduous pilgrimage may stretch between the land of our deliverance and our eternal home; our path of service may lead to many strange places, but God has ordained that certain things will provide the inspiration necessary for the journey. The greatest of these is the sacrament of the Lord's supper. Gratefully remembering His sacrifice, we meet around His table to handle reverently the emblems of His death. Every day we carry these in our hearts, and this we must continue to do until possession of our promised home is an accomplished reality. Then faith will be lost in sight. The communion service will be superseded by the marriage supper of the Lamb; we shall eat and drink together in the Kingdom of God. This great assurance strengthens us as we proceed on our way; these sacred emblems of the body and blood of our Lord mean far more to us than the bones of Joseph ever meant to Israel. We draw near to His table to whisper—

> Amazing love! how can it be
> That Thou, my God, shouldst die for me?

MOSES ... who tried to get out of a job
(EXODUS 3–4)

It is surprising what God can do with a man who thinks he is useless. Self-confidence is an advertisement of impotence; but a sense of insufficiency more often than not prepares the way to greatness. Moses was one of the greatest of men, yet he argued with God about the advisability of his being commissioned to deliver Israel. When Moses turned aside to see the burning bush, he heard a voice saying, "I am the God of thy father, the God of Abraham, the God of Isaac, and the God of Jacob ... I am come down to deliver Israel out of the hand of the Egyptians ... Come now therefore, and I will send thee unto Pharaoh" (Exod. 3:6, 8, 10).

ARGUMENT 1. *I'm a nobody*

"And Moses said unto God, Who am I, that I should go unto Pharaoh, and that I should bring forth the children of Israel out of Egypt? And God said, Certainly I will be with thee" (vv. 11-12). There is reason to believe that God had been specially training this man for the greater part of eighty years. Forty years had been spent in Pharaoh's palace, and a similar period had elapsed while he shepherded the flocks of his father-in-law. He had experimental knowledge of the military affairs of Egypt; he had enjoyed access to Egypt's palace; and through all the subsequent years had been patiently trained in the art of leading sheep. Undoubtedly he was the man fitted for the task.

ARGUMENT 2. *I have no message*

"And Moses said unto God, Behold when I come unto the children of Israel, and shall say unto them, The God of your fathers hath sent me unto you; and they shall say unto me, What is his name? What shall I say unto them?" (v. 13). In other words—O God, this is fantastic. I am a mere nobody, and I have nothing to say. How can I go to thy people? "And God said unto Moses, I AM THAT I AM: and he said, Thus shalt thou say unto the children of Israel, I AM hath sent me unto you" (vv. 13, 14). Moses had yet to learn that since the Commissioner was the eternally present—not the "*I was*" nor the "*I will be*," but the ever-present I AM, He would be always near to whisper the message needed. Most preachers who fail, do so because their preconceived notions crowd out God's whispers.

ARGUMENT 3. *The people are too difficult*

"And Moses answered and said, But, behold, they will not believe me, nor hearken unto my voice: for they will say, The Lord hath not appeared unto thee" (4:1). This statement was based upon a sound knowledge of human nature. The prediction of the anxious man came true, for the reactions of the people of God were exactly as he expected. They were difficult people indeed. But Moses had yet to discover that he was not expected to lead them alone. God would go with him into Egypt, and divine strength would be manifest in human weakness. No man is expected to be a hermit when he undertakes God's affairs.

ARGUMENT 4. *I am not a preacher*

"And Moses said unto the Lord, O my Lord, I am not eloquent, neither heretofore, nor since thou hast spoken unto thy servant: but I am slow of speech, and of a slow tongue" (4:10). Oh, Moses, you make us smile! You stated that you could not speak eloquently, and yet you seemed to be speaking very well indeed in the attempt to get out of a job! Whatever made you doubt your powers of expression? No wonder the Lord answered, "Who hath made man's mouth? ... Now therefore go, and I will be with thy mouth, and teach thee what thou shalt say" (vv. 11, 12). Successful preaching does not depend entirely upon human eloquence. A few halting words spoken in the power of the Holy Spirit can perform miracles, whereas the most elaborate oration may be a tinkling cymbal falling upon deaf ears.

ARGUMENT 5. *Send somebody else*

"And he said, O my Lord, send, I pray thee, by the hand of him whom thou wilt send. And the anger of the Lord was kindled against Moses ..." (vv. 13, 14). Send anybody, but don't send me. I am no use for that task. Poor old Moses, we can see his shaking head and hear his mutterings. No argument prevails against a call from heaven. Reluctantly Moses went down to Egypt, and God made him mighty.

> Oh to be nothing, nothing!
>   Simply to lie at His feet,
> A broken and emptied vessel,
>   For the Master's use made meet.
>
> Emptied that He might fill me,
>   As forth to His service I go;
> Broken, that so unhindered
>   His life through me might flow.

MOSES... who supplied Christ with a sermon illustration

(NUMBERS 21: 5-9)

During the month of October, 1852, a tragedy occurred at the Zoological Gardens in London. A man named Gurling, one of the keepers of the reptile house, was bitten by a cobra, and died within an hour. He had been to the farewell party of a man leaving for Australia, and had drunk too much gin. Some months previously he had been fascinated by a snake charmer's exhibition, and the scene was still before his confused mind when he returned to his snakes at the Zoo. First he took a Moroccan snake, and whirled it around his head. When his assistant cried, " For God's sake, put it back," he replied, " I'm inspired." He thereupon lifted a cobra, and in order to revive it from a stupor, put it inside his clothing. Later, when he held it in front of his face, he was immediately struck. As the blood trickled down his cheek, he sobered and cried for help. The assistant fled for his life. When others reached the dying man, they discovered that he had placed the snake back in its case, and was calmly sitting down. He said, " I am dead already." Gurling was rushed to hospital, where within an hour he paid the supreme price for his folly. His statement, " I am dead already," reminds us of a Bible story.

How Serious the Rebuke

The camp of Israel was filled with unrest. Faces were clouded, and the discussions among the people were most animated. The way to Canaan lay through difficult terrain, where serpents abounded. The barrenness of the surroundings matched the bleakness of their spirits. " And the people spake against God, and against Moses, Wherefore have ye brought us up out of Egypt to die in the wilderness? For there is no bread, neither is there any water; and our soul loatheth this light bread." Their biting criticisms of the great leader were unfair and sinful, and as these increased in intensity, God was very displeased. Until that moment, providential care had maintained a constant watch over the lurking serpents; now suddenly the undergrowth was filled with menace. " And the Lord sent fiery serpents among the people, and they bit the people; and much people of Israel died." The disaster was devastating in every respect, and as Gurling might have said, the men were dead even before they died.

How Simple the Remedy

"Therefore the people came to Moses, and said, We have sinned, for we have spoken against the Lord, and against thee; pray unto the Lord, that he take away the serpents from us. . . . And the Lord said unto Moses, Make thee a fiery serpent, and set it upon a pole: and it shall come to pass, that every one that is bitten, when he looketh upon it, shall live." As quickly as possible Moses obeyed, and ultimately the brazen serpent could be seen high above the heads of the people. Dying men were urged to look and live; and those who had been healed became messengers of good tidings, and helped other unfortunates. Within the scope of God's written word, profundity is wedded to simplicity. This is evident in the following details. (i) Israel urgently needed salvation. (ii) They could not save themselves. (iii) God provided a way of salvation, but He could not save Israel without the co-operation of the men in need. And as it was, so it is now.

How Sublime the Result

"Look and live; look and live." The cry reverberated throughout the camp. Men who chased the serpents paused to listen; despondent sufferers raised their heads; relatives who understood the importance of the great message, struggled to lift their loved ones to a viewpoint, and despair gave place to a new hope. The distant scene begins to fade, and instead we see a neat little sittingroom where the Lord interviewed Nicodemus. The preliminary conversation produced a theological question. The Saviour asserted that God the Father desired to transmit eternal life to men and women; but apparently this teaching could not be substantiated from the writings of the Fathers. "Master, how can these things be?" Christ replied, "And as Moses lifted up the serpent in the wilderness, even so must the Son of man be lifted up: That whosoever believeth in him should not perish, but have eternal life" (John 3:14, 15). It is clear that men in every age need God; that without His aid, they must die. Did any Israelite reject the invitation to look and live, preferring to rely upon his own ability to kill serpents? No! Such absurdities were left for people of later generations.

Look and live, my brother, live . . .
Look to Jesus, now, and live.

MOSES ... who preached about an eagle
(DEUTERONOMY 32: 11, 12)

Moses might have become an ardent ornithologist had not his other duties demanded so much attention. His journey through the wilderness and his lonely sojourns in the rugged heights of Mount Sinai provided excellent opportunities for bird-watching. It is not surprising that his sermons were enriched by illustrations discovered in nature. Probably he had looked down from some lofty crag and had been fascinated by the ways of an eagle. Perhaps the Lord arranged the display in order to enrich His servant's ministry.

How Strange are the Ways of God

"As an eagle stirreth up her nest.... So the Lord ..." The habits of eagles provide unfailing interest to bird lovers. The destruction of the nest high on the precipitous cliff is always a prelude to lessons in flying. The sticks are scattered, the home disturbed, and the tranquillity of the squawky youngsters rudely shattered as the wise old bird decides that her offspring should be prepared for the future. She realizes that unless they are pushed over the cliff they will never have the courage to go alone. Moses had no illusions on this matter, for he knew that God's ways resemble those of the queen of birds. Adversity is a great teacher.

How Watchful are the Ways of God

"As an eagle ... fluttereth over her young. ... So the Lord. ..." Ruthlessly, the parent bird pushes her chick over the edge of the precipice. Yet, even as he falls into the void, she hovers within inches of the flapping, frantic youngster. Wisdom and affection are manifest in every action. The anxious bird, trying so desperately to fly, probably forgets that his mother is near. Watching every move, she is ready instantly to rush to the rescue should danger threaten. "So the Lord. ..." Sometimes our troubles suggest that we are forsaken; but God is never far from His children.

How Careful are the Ways of God

"As an eagle ... spreadeth abroad her wings ... so the Lord. ..." Frantically the falling bird tries to arrest the downward rush, and his wings thrash the air. Relentlessly, the mother bird follows, and at the right moment her broad wings are spread out to form an aerial landing-stage for her chick. She knows that at the psychological moment she will need to move very quickly; there must be no accident, for the life of her child would be at stake. Surely Moses enjoyed preaching this sermon; for amid the dangers of life, the faithfulness of God remained unchanging. His care for Israel had never faltered.

How Reliable the Ways of God

"As an eagle . . . taketh her young . . . so the Lord. . . ." The mother eagle never failed to rescue her child. It would be inconceivable that she could ever abandon the falling bird. Isaiah had similar thoughts when he wrote, "Can a woman forget her sucking child, that she should not have compassion upon the son of her womb? yea, she may forget, *yet will I not forget thee*" (Isa. 49:15). The faithful dependability of God is beyond question; and happy are the people who trust in His care.

How Capable are the Ways of God

"As an eagle . . . beareth them on her wings. . . . So the Lord." If Moses really witnessed this thrilling scene, his eyes surely shone with delight. The youngsters would be carried safely into the heights, only to be thrown once again into mid-air. And so the procedure would be repeated, until slowly but surely the birds were taught to fly. Then, happy in the knowledge that her task had been perfectly executed, the parent eagle flew away with her brood. Alas, similar kindness had been lavished in vain upon the children of Israel; for having been instructed in the great ways of righteousness, "Jeshurun waxed fat, and kicked" (v. 15). Moses proceeded to outline the sorry state of Israel when he said, "Of the Rock that begat thee thou art unmindful, and hast forgotten God that formed thee" (v. 18). The captive Israelites in Babylon cried, "If I forget thee . . . let my right hand forget her cunning . . ." (Psa. 137:5). Gratitude begets praise; ingratitude is the mother of indifference. Lord, give me a good memory!

JOSHUA . . . and his prophetic symbolism
(JOSHUA 4: 3–20)

Joshua and Paul had much in common, and their discussions concerning spiritual life would have delighted the hearts of all Christians. They studied in the same theological seminary, only Joshua belonged to an earlier generation of students! Yet each in his own way wrote a thesis on the same subject, and both efforts gained a degree in heaven's university. Joshua bequeathed to us his treatise on spiritual warfare, and Paul did likewise. Either one could have written the other's book; and apart from a few historical details, the respective writings would have remained the same. Joshua took his people through Jordan, and then led them into Canaan. Paul spoke of identification with Christ in His death, and then expounded the secrets of spiritual triumphs in heavenly places. The epistle to the Ephesians is the revised version of the book of Joshua!

Buried with Christ

"And Joshua set up twelve stones in the midst of Jordan, in the place where the feet of the priests which bare the ark of the covenant stood: and they are there unto this day" (Josh. 4:9). Israel had been redeemed from Egypt, and after spending lamentable years wandering in the wilderness, were about to realize their deepest longings. Ahead lay the promised land, with all its glorious possibilities. Yet the path to victory was an ordered path. Certain ritual had to be observed, for this experience was destined to instruct men in all ages. Solemnly, Joshua commanded his men to lift twelve stones from the bed of the river; and when this had been done, he took another twelve stones from the bank, and deliberately set them up in the river-bed—probably in the very holes from which the first twelve had been taken. Then with dignified tread he climbed the bank, and turned to watch the waters of the river covering the stones of witness. There is something strangely suggestive about all this, and we remember Paul's words, " Know ye not, that so many of us as were baptized into Jesus Christ were baptized into his death? Therefore we are buried with him by baptism into death: that like as Christ was raised up from the dead by the glory of the Father, even so we also should walk in newness of life. For if we have been planted together in the likeness of his death, we shall be also in the likeness of his resurrection: Knowing this, that our old man is crucified with him, that the body of sin might be destroyed, that henceforth we should not serve sin " (Rom. 6:3-7).

Raised with Christ

Joshua commanded, "Take you hence out of the midst of Jordan . . . twelve stones, and ye shall carry them over with you, and leave them in the lodging place, where ye shall lodge this night. . . . And the people came up out of Jordan on the tenth day of the first month . . . and those twelve stones . . . did Joshua pitch in Gilgal" (vv. 3, 20). The sun shone down on the rugged memorial, and every onlooker remembered the identical erection in the Jordan. There, the symbols of the old Israel had been buried; but here, at Gilgal, stood the emblems of the new Israel. The people had crossed to Canaan, and with God as their Leader, anything was possible. Paul would have appreciated that scene, for in after days, with similar truths in his mind, he wrote "He hath raised us up together, and made us sit together in heavenly places in Christ Jesus" (Ephes. 2:6). Although Israel had been brought safely from Egypt, their redemption could not be perfected while they remained wandering in the wilderness. Even so, a Christian may rejoice in deliverance from the bondage of sin, but while carnality keeps his feet in paths of the self-life, the greatest features of God's provision will be unrealized.

Enthroned with Christ

Led by their new captain (Josh. 5:15) Israel marched against Jericho, and the prospects of a glorious future thrilled their souls. Nothing but sin could interfere with their onward march of triumph. We can almost hear Joshua borrowing the words of his New Testament brother, and saying to Israel, "Finally, my brethren, be strong in the Lord, and in the power of his might. Put on the whole armour of God, that ye may be able to stand against the wiles of the devil. For we wrestle not against flesh and blood, but against principalities, against powers, against the rulers of the darkness of this world, against spiritual wickedness in high places" (Ephes. 6:10-12).

Yet he who would conquer in Canaan, must first die in Jordan. The man who said, "I die daily" was able to say also, "I can do all things through Christ which strengtheneth me" (Phil. 4:13).

THE FIVE KINGS ... who were in a hole
(Joshua 10: 16)

They were very foolish, for in time of danger they walked into a cave, and a cave can be a dead end! Yet their stupidity had been apparent for days; they seemed to have developed a habit of getting into a hole! One would have thought that five kings would have had more sense. They did not consider that it was much easier to get into a hole than to get out of one. They had illustrious names. Adonizedec, king of Jerusalem; Hoham, king of Hebron; Piram, king of Jarmuth; Japhia, king of Lachish, and Debir, king of Eglon. Far be it from us to criticize the descriptions of these ancient monarchs, but history suggests that their titles were inadequate. At the risk of inviting criticism, let us attend a posthumous christening service!

The King of Unrighteousness

Every Canaanite knew that the children of Israel were on the march. Their intrepid leader, Joshua, was filled with the wisdom of God, and already his exploits had terrorized the border cities of the land. Jericho and Ai had fallen, and it was only a matter of time before the invaders would advance toward other centres. It was also stated that the God of these strange people loved righteousness and hated iniquity. This was a holy war against the abominations of the Canaanite cities. One royal outpost had capitulated, and by means of trickery had made peace with the invaders. The king of Jerusalem heard the news, and scowled. He had no thought for his iniquitous systems; he shed no tears for his sins. He thought only of resistance; and, summoning four other monarchs, he prepared to go forth in defence of his kingdom. Had he honestly abandoned his sin, he might have avoided getting into a hole!

The King of Unreasonableness

"Come up unto me," he said, "and help me, that we may smite Gibeon; for it hath made peace with Joshua, and with the children of Israel" (v. 4). This was poor military strategy; the real danger lay in the camp of Israel, and not in the surrendered city of Canaan. It was suicidal to sacrifice valiant fighting men on the altar of personal feuds. It was not necessary to warn other wavering cities, for these were joining in the battle of vengeance. This stupidity demonstrated that the Canaanite heart-disease had spread upwards! They were not only evil; they were prepared to defend their wickedness. Obviously they were heading for a hole!

The King of Unrepentance

"And the Lord discomforted them before Israel . . . and chased them. . . . And it came to pass . . . that the Lord cast down great stones from heaven upon them . . . they were more which died with hailstones than they whom the children of Israel slew with the sword" (vv. 10, 11). And still there appeared no sign of repentance. The Gibeonites had made mention of the God of Israel, and even though fear had played a major part in their deliberations, at least some measure of faith had been produced. These five kings relied upon their self-sufficiency. It is not for us to decide whether or not their repentance would have obtained pardon—the fact remains that they preferred to get into a hole than to kneel to pray.

The King of Unpleasantness

Everything had gone wrong. Their armies had been defeated on the field of battle; their cause had perished, and their future was fraught with great peril. Realizing their need of a refuge, the five kings ran toward the hills. Possibly one of them knew the location of a cave, and thought it would offer a respite. He led the way, and thus it has been written, "But these five kings fled, and hid themselves in a cave at Makkedah." Amid the gloom of that cavern it would have been impossible to identify this fourth king, for by some optical phenomenon all five faces seemed alike. They were all in a hole! They had made shipwreck of life, and were now clutching at straws!

The King of Uselessness

They cowered in the far end of their cavern; they heard the huge stones being rolled into position at the mouth of the cave (vv. 17, 18). Then, as silence reigned in the prison, one man crept forward to reconnoitre the position. The entrance had been blocked. Too late, the stricken men discovered there was no other exit; they were caught like rats in a trap. And during all the years that followed, the pile of stones reminded travellers of the cave which had become a grave. Five foolish men had slipped into a hole, and had failed to climb out. Poor fellows—the hole was as deep as eternity. Joshua should have placed an inscription on the tomb. "Keep on God's highway, and avoid cul-de-sacs."

DAGON . . . who reappears in other temples
(1 Samuel 5: 4)

The priests were dumbfounded; their faces were masks of incredulity! They were absolutely horrified as they surveyed the wreckage scattered across the floor of their sacred house. Such vandalism had never been known. ". . . behold, Dagon was fallen upon his face to the ground before the ark of the Lord; and the head of Dagon and both the palms of his hands were cut off upon the threshold; only the stump of Dagon was left to him." The ark of the God of Israel was silent, sombre, and still; but every Philistine realized that its apparent impotence was misleading. That ark had struck terror to the heart of their god—that is, if he had a heart!

Proposition 1. *How strong. God is quite capable of looking after Himself*

The conquest of Israel and the resultant capture of the sacred ark had made the Philistines delirious with joy. Their ancient enemies were now at their mercy; their god was in captivity. Dagon would be triumphant for ever; the captured ark had been placed at his feet. It was wonderful; and the heathen danced for joy. But "when they arose early on the morrow, behold, Dagon was fallen upon his face to the earth before the ark of the Lord. And they took Dagon, and set him in his place again" (v. 3). When the god fell the second time, the priests were demoralized and lost their desire to serve in his temple. Their position was intolerable. The power of the captured box beggared description. Had a true prophet been present, his eyes would have smiled from a face grimly inscrutable. The priests should have known on the first morning that Dagon's tumble was but a precursor of coming tragedy. God was very capable of fighting His own battles wherever the enemy was found.

Proposition 2. *How sensitive. Sin can stay His hand*

It is sometimes difficult to recognize God's invincibility when temporary defeat overwhelms His cause. If the ark represented eternal might, why were the Philistines permitted to seize it? The answer to that question might have been found in the sanctuary. "Now the sons of Eli were sons of Belial; they knew not the Lord . . . the sin of the young men was very great . . . for men abhorred the offering of the Lord" (1 Sam. 2:12, 17). Deliberate sin had ruined Israel; their respect for the ark amounted solely to idolatry. Thus God decided to teach His people a most painful lesson. He permitted the conquest by the Philistines, that in defeat Israel might learn the lessons which they ignored in victory. These are age-long principles. Neither man nor movement need fear when their cause is just in the sight of God. " No good thing will he withhold from those who walk uprightly."

PROPOSITION 3. *How significant. God never finally forsakes His people*

Dagon's fall was followed by other disasters, for wherever the Philistines took the ark, the people were smitten by death and disease. Ultimately the wise men diagnosed the cause of their trouble, and advised that the ark should be returned to Israel. Yet, to remove any doubt in the matter, the ark was placed upon a new cart, to which were harnessed two milch cows whose calves were left in the stall. " And the kine took the straight way to Beth-shemesh, and went along the highway, lowing as they went, and turned not aside to the right hand or to the left . . . " (1 Sam. 6:12). Thus God returned to His people, who by all known laws had forfeited the right of His favour. God's kindness is always greater than man's sin, and every phase of religious history demonstrates the fact. God permitted His people to go into Egypt, but He brought them out again. God allowed the Babylonians to subjugate Israel; He allowed the stricken nation to remain in captivity for seventy intolerable years, but in the fullness of time He brought them home again. Mankind may grieve and forsake God, but God never forsakes His children.

PROPOSITION 4. *How safe I may be if my Dagon is smashed!*

" He that dwelleth in the secret place of the most High shall abide under the shadow of the Almighty " (Psa. 91:1). Dagon's mutilation suggests that God enjoys select company. He can be exceedingly jealous, and resents the presence of other deities. I cannot expect His blessing when my own idols are permitted to stand on their feet! If I emulate the example of the priests of Ashdod, if I ignore God's initial warning, His second stroke will be far heavier than the first. It is always easier and wiser for man to smash his own idols—this relieves God of a task.

DAVID . . . and his habit of slaying giants
(1 SAMUEL 17: 49)

The scene was awe-inspiring, for the man-mountain had appeared again from the tents of the Philistines. He sneered and asked, "Why are ye come out to set your battle in array? am not I a Philistine, and ye servants to Saul? choose you a man for you, and let him come down to me. If he be able to fight with me, and to kill me, then will we be your servants: but if I prevail against him, and kill him, then shall ye be our servants, and serve us . . . I defy the armies of Israel this day" (vv. 9, 10). And as young David heard the challenge, he looked expectantly toward his countrymen. Surely this blasphemous heathen should be taught a lesson. What, is there no man willing to fight him? Then I will. It was unbelievable; even Israel stood aghast. A mere boy had performed the impossible. They surged forward to reap the reward of his deed. They overtook and slew many Philistines; but Goliath had strange relations who lived to fight another day.

The Giant of Regal Fury

Saul was desperately angry; hidden fires smouldered within his breast. This upstart had bewitched and stolen the hearts of Israel. What were they singing? "Saul has slain his thousands, and David his ten thousands" (18:7). Bah! Jealousy made him furious; his hands clenched at his side. David was a menace. The boy's smiles were maddening; his music thrilled the soul, but everything was wrong, and suddenly the volcanic powers erupted in Saul's breast. "And Saul cast the javelin; for he said, I will smite David even to the wall with it. . . . And David behaved himself wisely in all his ways; and the Lord was with him" (18:11-14). Saul repeatedly revealed the same inexcusable ferocity of purpose, but on each occasion David overcame bitterness with kindness. Then another giant came forward.

The Giant of Personal Revenge

Poor David had been driven from all his friends. He was homeless, and went in danger of his life; but God smiled upon the fugitive. The camp of Saul was wrapped in slumber, for the men, weary with the pursuits of the day, had lain down to rest. Even the sentries slept at their posts. David smiled in the shadows. A little care, and his enemy would be at his mercy. David calmly watched the camp, and deliberately planned his line of approach to the royal tent. Then he began the most perilous journey of his career. It was done; his enemy lay at his feet. David heard the suggestions of evil, "Smite him now, and remove your enemy. Israel will acclaim your deed. Has not God delivered him into your hands? This is the chance of a lifetime. Seize it." The youthful captain shook his head. King Saul was the Lord's anointed. David silently severed a piece of the sleeper's skirt, and then disappeared into the blackness of the night. He had conquered another giant. The reactions in the realm of evil were very considerable; this David was a great warrior. Was there another volunteer to challenge this Israelite? Certainly, a giant was already on his feet.

The Giant of Tormenting Guilt

He was clever—ruthlessly clever. He avoided open conflict with this dynamic fighter, for he knew David had to be trapped. Were there openings in the royal armour? Were there any weak spots in the king's rugged defences? Could any dart pierce to the heart of the invincible? What about a little bewitching beauty? What about an illegitimate affection? Could this impregnable human citadel be destroyed by fire—the fire of unholy passion, kindled by a spark of lust? It was worth trying. The giant planned his campaign, and David was soon fighting for his life. Apollyon had hands of toughened steel, and those hands were choking him. His eyes blurred; his heart was bursting. The devil of lust had ruined his fighting qualities. Adultery, villainy, murder, had filled the music of his soul with vibrating discords. He reeled back under the pressure of the enemy, and was haunted by the memory of his disgraceful conduct. A man lay in his grave; the fair name of a beautiful wife had become eternally stained; he himself was guilty before God. And Giant Guilt sneered at his helpless victim. It was the monster's first mistake, for it gave David an opportunity to get on his knees. The guilty man prayed (Psa. 51), and the oppressor had the shock of his life. The battle continued for a long time, but the end was no longer in doubt. Ultimately the giant was overcome. He had been so near to triumph, but had thrown away his chances. David never gave him another opportunity, for he knew these giants, and liked them as much as they liked him.

SAUL ... who seemed to be hypnotized
(1 SAMUEL 19: 19-24)

Dear David,
It's strange that we are thinking of you, when we should be thinking of Saul; but that's just the way of things. You two always seemed to be getting in each other's way, and whenever we read of King Saul, we expect you to appear on the page. No, no, do not misunderstand us; we are glad, very glad, for action was always to be expected when you and Saul came together. You are not too busy to answer a few questions? Good. You remember those troublesome days when Saul hunted you from pillar to post; when life was a nightmare; when death threatened to overtake you at any moment. Did you laugh when your wife put an image in your bed, covered it with a sheet, and then tucked in it as if she were caring for her husband? No wonder Saul was mad when he discovered what she had done.

How Inviting

We have often read, "So David fled, and escaped, and came to Samuel to Ramah, and told him all that Saul had done to him. And he and Samuel went and dwelt at Naioth" (1 Sam. 19:18). David, that verse appeals to us a great deal, for Samuel was the mouthpiece of God. Amid all the decadent conditions of his day, he stood for truth and goodness. To be near him was to stand in the Lord's presence. His home was a sanctuary; his smile a benediction. You felt safe with him. God's man was your friend; he was a refuge in the storm. We know how you felt, for we have often acted similarly. When ugly circumstances followed us day after day, we fled for refuge to Another who was also God's Man.

How Irresistible

Were you just a little scared when the party of soldiers came to take you away? Did you tremble, and look expectantly toward your kind benefactor? Were you amazed when he quietly smiled; when "The Spirit of God was upon them, and they prophesied." David, weren't you astonished when this procedure was twice repeated? Samuel, assured, dignified, stood at your side. His eyes were pools of inscrutable mystery; the smile playing about his lips held just a trace of mockery and scorn. Who were these stupid men, that they should challenge the authority of the Most High? Yes, the messengers of Saul were swayed by eternal powers; they spoke words of praise, and extolled the name of the Almighty.

David, you knew a thing or two, didn't you, when you took shelter with Samuel?

How Invincible

And then king Saul arrived (v. 22). Wasn't he stupid! Yes, he would show Samuel that other people as well as he could act and speak with authority. "Men, seize the scoundrel David, and brook no interference!" And Samuel's eyes merely flickered. Imperceptibly the lines around his mouth deepened; his beard twitched, as if suppressed mirth wanted to break forth. Gravely the prophet inclined his head, and behold, " . . . the Spirit of God was upon Saul also, and he went on, and prophesied, until he came to Naioth in Ramah. And he stripped off his clothes also, and prophesied before Samuel in like manner, and lay down naked all that day and all that night. Wherefore they say, Is Saul also among the prophets?" And still Samuel watched him. David, do you know what the worldly wise people of our age would say about that event? They would declare that Samuel was a hypnotist; that king Saul was impressionable and went under! Not that it matters, for if God desired, He could paralyse an army of kings!

How Inspiring

What happened after the demonstration ended? It must have been funny to see Saul waking up. Surely he was disconcerted when he discovered his need of clothing. Was he any wiser, or did he become morose and sullen? He was a strange man. But, David, we cannot understand why you fled from Samuel. You were very fearful when you found Jonathan and said, "What have I done? What is mine iniquity? and what is my sin before thy father, that he seeketh my life?" (20:1). Of course, we may be all wrong in our thinking, but it seems to us that since the presence of Samuel afforded glorious protection, you would have been well advised to remain with him. Were you afraid that he might die and leave you at the mercy of your enemy? What a pity you are so far away, David. You could tell us so much. Anyhow, we have a Saviour who will never die. We fled for refuge to Him, and felt so much at home in His presence, that we decided to stay for ever. What do you think of that, David?

BARZILLAI . . . who went home to wait for God
(2 SAMUEL 19: 33-37)

Dear Barzillai,

You are one of the not-so-well-known characters of the ancient writings, for your story is hidden in history—but we have found you out! You didn't like a lot of publicity, and perhaps even now you will shrink from being brought into the limelight. Accept our apologies, noble sir, and if our actions seem to offend, grant an indulgence. We like you; we like you a lot, for in that wise old head of yours you possess much wisdom. Again and again we have read the brief record of your exploits, and it seems to us that you passed through four definite phases. Forgive us if we seem to be chopping up your story; but, dear friend, we are preachers. I suppose that proves one thing or another. I don't know which!

Your Personal Regard

We have been told that when David fled from the rebellion of Absalom, you with others, " Brought beds, and basons, and earthen vessels, and wheat, and barley, and flour, and parched corn, and beans, and lentiles, and parched pulse. And honey, and butter, and sheep, and cheese of kine, for David, and for the people that were with him, to eat: for they said, The people is hungry, and weary, and thirsty, in the wilderness " (2 Sam. 17:27-29). Nice work, Barzillai! You thought of everything in that hour of emergency. In these modern days people would have taken a collection of tinned foods, and would have forgotten the tin opener! We have often considered your liking for David. Surely you thought a great deal of your master, for at the time of your allegiance the outlook was gloomy. We admire loyalty and faithfulness, and your glorious deed became an immortal example. Well done, old man. We are proud of you.

Your Persistent Refusal

How we would have loved to see David's face when you disappointed him. Oh, Barzillai! He had planned to give you the time of your life. What a present for your eightieth birthday—a royal present, too ; and you refused it. How long did David try to persuade you to alter your mind? Old friend, we know many people who would have jumped at the chance to accompany David to the palace, to live in the lap of luxury. The soft lights and sweet music of the kingly household would ravish their hearts, and on no consideration would they refuse a king's offer. We can still hear David saying, "Come thou over with me, and I will feed thee with me in Jerusalem (19:33)—and you shook your head.

Your Potent Realization

"I am this day fourscore years old: and can I discern between good and evil? can thy servant taste what I eat or what I drink? can I hear any more the voice of singing men and singing women? wherefore then should thy servant be yet a burden unto my lord the king? . . . Let thy servant I pray thee, turn back again, that I may die in mine own city, and be buried by the grave of my father and of my mother." You crafty old man—you were an expert diplomat. Even David could not have been offended at the refusal, for your arguments were unassailable. You could not hear—you could not taste—quite right, Barzillai, but you could see, and there was a great deal to be seen in David's presence. But you were looking elsewhere, your eyes were on eternity. "How long have I to live?" you asked, and at the same time you could have supplied an approximate answer. "A few weeks, a few months, but at most a few years. Should I waste my precious moments on the frivolities of earth, when soon I shall commence the important journey into the hereafter? No, David, I am going home to attend to the most important business in life."

Your Peaceful Readiness

Old friend, we would like to ask a question. How long had you to wait before the call came? We see you sitting peacefully at home; we appreciate the deep content filling your soul. Your lifetime of ready service was a source of constant satisfaction; your opportunities had not been lost. The unknown road ahead did not fill you with misgivings. Your people had gone that way, and their Guide would soon be coming to guide their aged son. Of course, you could not tell us about your funeral; but we believe it was a procession of quiet dignity. It wasn't a funeral, but a home-going and a reunion. You were ready for the eternal call, and God was proud to welcome you. Fortunate man! How we wish that all men would learn from your story. We struggle and scheme, we save and plan, and so often forget that a similar call could come to us at any moment. Oh, Barzillai, we are all mixed up. We say, "a bird in the hand is worth two in the bush," but that is not always true. A mansion in Immanuel's land would be worth a city in this land. Barzillai, we have much to learn!

JOAB ... who lacked staying power

(1 KINGS 1: 7)

Joab was one of the greatest of David's servants, and it will ever be a source of regret that this fine man failed in the end. There are details which suggest that provocation forced the valiant warrior into error; but whether or not this is true, he who had run his race so well, failed near the winning post! There are many instances of this man's chivalrous conduct, but the following quotations will provide a most suggestive study.

His Great Fame

"And David reigned over all Israel; and David executed judgment and justice unto all his people. And Joab the son of Zeruiah was over the host" (1 Sam. 8:15, 16). We are not conversant with all the details concerning the promotion of this intrepid warrior, but it may be safely assumed that his acts of bravery, his ability to lead men, and his unwavering courage, brought him to prominence. David recognized his greatness, and conferred upon him the honour which every Israelite coveted. Joab's subsequent record vindicated David's decision.

His Great Friendship

Joab knew the details concerning the flight of Prince Absalom, but prudently minded his own business. Yet as the years passed, he recognized "... the soul of king David longed to go forth unto Absalom: for he was comforted concerning the death of Amnon, seeing he was dead" (2 Sam. 13:39). Daily the wise and friendly commander watched his royal master, and ultimately decided to arrange a reconciliation. His commission to the wise woman of Tekoah has been previously studied. (See *Bible Pinnacles*, p. 43.) It is sufficient now to remember that through the kindly intervention of this thoughtful man, David's sadness was banished. The king did not act very graciously in the matter of Absalom's return, but at least Joab had done his best.

His Great Faithfulness

Utterly unselfish and unquestionably loyal, Joab proceeded to do his duty, and on one notable occasion refused to press home his victorious attack on an enemy stronghold until his master had arrived, to be credited with the success of the campaign. Probably this would rank as his greatest act of self-denial. Joab desired David to have the pre-eminence in all things. A runner was despatched with news of the impending victory, and the king was urged to come immediately, to receive the praises of his people (2 Sam. 12: 26-31). This act of self-effacement deserved the greatest honour in the kingdom.

His Great Fearlessness

It is not true to say that love is blind. This man adored his master, but he was able to see the faults in David's attitude. Probably it required far more courage to rebuke the king than it did to go forth against an invading army. The wounds of a friend are faithful, and on several occasions the brave general quietly rebuked his monarch. David resented these admonitions, but subsequent events proved Joab to be right. After the death of Absalom, David's sorrow grieved the people, and it was Joab's advice which prevented serious repercussions. Later, the king stupidly embarked upon a course of action displeasing to God. It was suicidal; but only Joab had the courage to oppose the royal command. His objections were over-ruled, and as a result seventy thousand people perished. The king's stupidity was unimaginable, but alas, David had wandered far from God.

His Great Folly

Let us not be too severe in our condemnation of this weakening soldier. The increasing folly of the aged king, and the whispers that Solomon had been commissioned to execute the great general (1 Kings 2: 3-6), were sufficient to disillusion any man. Mistrust and intrigue affected the frustrated leader, and the renegade Adonijah found him to be fertile soil in which to plant seeds of rebellion (1 Kings 1: 7). Joab was like a wonderful racehorse whose stout heart and untiring legs had brought it to within inches of the winning post. Modern men would say that, after running a grand race, " he was pipped on the post." What a shame! It would have been better had he retired from the political scene before he blemished his record of service. We should learn from the story, and be determined to run with patience the race that is set before us, looking unto Jesus, the Author and Finisher of our faith (Heb. 12: 1-2).

OBADIAH ... whose widow complained
(1 KINGS 18: 5–16 ; 2 KINGS 4: 1–7)

The writings of Josephus suggest an interesting possibility in regard to two Old Testament personalities. Supported by other authorities, the historian declares that the widow whose pot of oil was miraculously increased by the prophet Elisha, was none other than Obadiah's widow. "For they say that the widow of Obadiah, Ahab's steward, came to Elisha and said, that he was not ignorant how her husband had preserved the prophets that were to be slain by Jezebel, the wife of Ahab ; for she said, that he hid a hundred of them, and had borrowed money for their maintenance, and that, after her husband's death, she and her children were carried away to be made slaves by the creditors ; and she desired of him to have mercy upon her on account of what her husband did, and afford her some assistance. And when he asked her what she had in the house, she said, 'Nothing but a very small quantity of oil in a cruse.' So the prophet bid her go away, and borrow a great many empty vessels of her neighbours, and when she had shut her chamber door, to pour the oil into them all: for that God would fill them full." A footnote to this quotation reads, "That this woman who cried to Elisha, and who in our Bible is styled 'the wife of one of the sons of the prophets,' was no other than the widow of Obadiah, the good steward of Ahab, is confirmed by the Chaldee paraphrase and by the Rabbins and others ..." (*Antiquities of the Jews*. Book nine, chapter four, para. two). If these statements are founded on fact, then the ancient account becomes increasingly interesting.

An Exceptional Ministry—Inspiring

King Ahab was very angry, and his inflammatory temper had turned interviews into nightmare experiences for all his subjects. The country had been ravaged by unprecedented drought, and disaster threatened the nation. The irate monarch cursed the prophet Elijah, and vowed that he should be executed. "Obadiah, where are you?" and the anxious prime minister bowed before his master. "Go into the land, unto all fountains of water, and unto all brooks ; peradventure we may find grass to save the horses and mules alive, that we lose not all the beasts. So they divided the land between them" (1 Kings 18:5, 6). Had Ahab known that his chief executive officer was at that very time sheltering a company of the hated prophets of God, Obadiah would have been instantly slain. This is the highlight of Old Testament secret service; for in the very shadow of the palace, the prime minister nightly risked his life to serve the cause of God.

An Expensive Ministry—Impoverishing

His statement to Elijah, "Was it not told my lord what I did when Jezebel slew the prophets of the Lord, how I hid an hundred men of the Lord's prophets by fifty in a cave, and fed them with bread and water?" (v. 13) provides a window through which we may view the activities of those dread nights. Under cover of darkness, hunted saints were quietly led along mountain paths to the shelter of a remote cave. Yet every enterprise of this nature needed money, and Obadiah financed the venture. It would appear that all his savings were sacrificed, and that ultimately he had to borrow money or abandon his efforts. Some teachers have declared that his secret endeavours evidenced a lack of courage; that he should have boldly confronted Ahab, confessing his faith in God. Yet such an act would have invited disaster not only to the indiscreet man, but to many others who were dependent upon his endeavours. It will be to his everlasting credit that, rather than abandon his friends, he willingly spent all he possessed.

An Exasperating Ministry—Implemented

If we may accept the teaching of ancient writers, then in after days, when Obadiah had died, his widow, impoverished and in danger of slavery, cried to Elisha for assistance. She claimed that the prophet was fully conversant with the details of her misfortune; that such a state of affairs had been brought about by her husband's loyalty to the cause of God. Surely something ought to be done about the matter. And Elisha smiled. He might have said, " For God is not unrighteous to forget your work and labour of love, which ye have shewed toward his name, in that ye have ministered to the saints, and do minister " (Heb. 6:10). The woman obeyed the commands of God's servant, and soon had sufficient money to meet all her needs. Thus did God reward the faithfulness of His children. Obadiah never lived to see the realization of his dreams, for his greatest prayers were answered after his death. God is no man's debtor, and money and time invested in His work will return amazing dividends.

ELISHA . . . and the slaughter of the innocents
(2 KINGS 2: 23, 24)

"And Elisha went up from thence unto Bethel: and as he was going up by the way, there came forth little children out of the city, and mocked him, and said unto him, Go up, thou bald head ; go up, thou bald head. And he turned back, and looked on them, and cursed them in the name of the Lord. And there came forth two she bears out of the wood, and tare forty and two children of them. And he went from thence to mount Carmel." At first, this account seems foreign to the nature of God. That He who said "Suffer little children to come unto me, for of such is the kingdom of heaven" should ever fulfil a curse in allowing wild animals to slaughter innocent boys and girls, seems completely inconceivable. Such a thing never happened.

The Determined Rabble

The word used in the Hebrew text is not exclusively used to describe adolescents, and there is reason to believe that a more correct translation would be "youths." The idea that the prophet was being followed by a crowd of children who had just left school—a crowd of mischievous boys and girls who playfully teased the stranger—is very far from the truth. This rabble was composed of unruly young men who had banded themselves together and had followed the young prophet along the road. They hated righteousness, and resented interference from any spiritual leader. They recognized that the teachings of Elisha were diametrically opposed to all their sensual delights. It is important to remember that their city was a centre of idolatry. Bethel, the House of God, had degenerated into a centre of heathenism, where men worshipped idols and had become a law unto themselves. When the prophet of the Highest appeared, the young fellows sneered at his approach, and went forth to express their hatred.

The Dastardly Remarks

"They mocked him, and said unto him, Go up, thou bald head ; go up, thou bald head." It is well to consider that unless misfortune had robbed the young prophet of his hair, it was most unlikely that at this stage of his life he was bald. Yet the crowd repeated the cry, and found in their taunts a certain amount of pleasure. To the casual reader, it would appear that the man of God was somewhat irritable that morning, and to be teased by the young innocents was more than he could endure. But the young men were not referring to the feeble efforts of an old "bald head" trying to climb a hill, but rather to the homecall of Elijah, who had just ascended into heaven. Students will probably know that the worst blasphemy may be found in their cries. It has been said that a fair translation of the text would be, "Go up, go up to heaven with thy master, thou ... prophet of Jehovah." They were cursing him; and however unpleasant it may be even to read such words, it is necessary to do so in order to understand the disaster which suddenly overwhelmed the crowd of sinners. The despicable mob resented Elisha's presence in the vicinity; they cursed him and scorned his authority, and probably contemplated violence. Then suddenly the prophet turned and looked at them.

The Devastating Response

"And he cursed them in the name of the Lord." He knew that these great sinners would become the fathers of the next generation, and realized also that the whole of his ministry was in jeopardy. Elisha had only recently succeeded to his master's office, and the nation had yet to be taught that he was the Lord's anointed. Such blatant sin demanded rebuke. Yet apart from any curse announced by Elisha, the young people were personally responsible for the disaster which overwhelmed them. The two bears had been frightened. Probably thinking that their young were in danger, they followed their natural instincts and went forth to attack the enemy. Panic spread among the screeching crowd and, utterly confused, the youths rushed in all directions. "And the bears tare forty and two of them." It is hard to decide whether the victims were actually killed or merely wounded. The man of God watched the scene and, when the survivors fled to the nearby city, when the bears ambled back to the woods, he probably bowed his head in holy reverence. The God of Elijah was with him; there was no need to fear. And wrapping his mantle around him, he proceeded calmly on his way.

JABEZ ... the giant among dwarfs
(1 Chronicles 4: 9, 10)

"And these were of the father of Etam; Jezreel, and Ishma, and Idbash: and the name of their sister was Hazelelponi: And Penuel the father of Gedor, and Ezer the father of Hushah. These are the sons of Hur ... and Ashur the father of Tekoa had two wives, Helah and Naarah. And Naarah bare him Ahuzam, and Hepher, and Temeni, and Haahashtari ... And the sons of Helah were, Zareth, and Jezoar, and Ethnan. And Coz begat Anub, and Zobebah ..."—Oh, Mr. Historian, they are enough! We are perspiring already. Historical records can be stimulating and exciting; but when you must write things such as these, oh dear! Weren't you bored when you could only record that people lived in a certain village; that they bore children, and then died? We are thankful you refused to leave your task, for among the ancient dwarfs a giant appeared. Weren't you thrilled to find him in the records? A few words were sufficient to describe other people; yet for Jabez you had much more to say. He was an oasis in a desert! We are refreshed!

Grief Allowed

"And Jabez was more honourable than his brethren: and his mother called his name Jabez, saying, *Because I bare him with sorrow.*" We are not certain that this boy lived up to his reputation; that his name expressed his nature: but we know that he commenced his earthly journey in adversity. The historian did not supply the details which we seem to need, and we can only imagine the grievous trials which attended the birth of Jabez. The growing child surely wondered why his mother was sad. Did he reflect her gloom? These things were permitted in order to produce within the boy a desire for deeper spiritual experiences. He lived in a world of little people, where sometimes even God longed for fellowship with a real man!

Greatness Acquired

"And Jabez was more honourable than his brethren." We cannot read the mind of the writer concerning the matter, but one thing is certain—Jabez was a giant among pigmies! His greatness was a rare orchid grown from the soil of adversity. His sadness begat dignity, and suffering encouraged sympathetic understanding of the problems of other people. Jabez became spiritually famous. He was the man of God among men; the giant among dwarfs; an honoured saint where spirituality was at a premium.

Godliness Appealing

"And Jabez called on the God of Israel, saying, Oh that thou wouldest bless me indeed, and enlarge my coast, and that thine hand might be with me, and that thou wouldest keep me from evil, that it may not grieve me!" This prayer of Jabez repays investigation. It divides into four sections, for he asked the Lord to bless, to help, to guide, and to save. And shining through all the fervent longings of this unknown Bible character was an intense longing for godliness. His desire to be kept from evil might be interpreted as a yearning for protection against enemies. On the other hand, Jabez might have feared sin more than he feared his fellow men. He believed in the power of prayer. He believed that the fervent prayer of a righteous man availed much. His hope lay in God, and in no other; and it was this remarkable faith which increased his stature. The daily prayer arose from his honourable heart, and while other people pursued carnal ambitions, Jabez knelt in the secret place.

Gladness Assured

"And God granted him that which he requested." We cannot be sure whether or not the city of Jabez was named after this great man (2:55), but we are justified in assuming that the Lord prospered his efforts. Alas, the faithful historian returned too quickly to the monotonous recording of the uneventful. We wish he had provided more details concerning the prayers of Jabez. How did the Lord answer those prayers, and what were the reactions of the Israelite? The rest of the story is wrapped in silence, and we are left to imagine the mighty triumphs wrought through the intercessions of the prayer warrior. Answered prayers beget within hearts a sense of deep gratitude, and of surging joy. Jabez soon discovered that his sighing was turning to song; his grief to gladness. "Then was his tongue filled with singing, and his lips with mirth." Apparently he was not a great preacher, nor an organizing genius; and he never became famous on the field of battle. Prayer alone made him great. Effective intercession gilded his name with immortality. Such men have saved the world. Such people are numbered among God's aristocracy.

JEHOSHAPHAT ... who was known by his prayer

(2 CHRONICLES 18: 31)

Superb magnificence overshadowed the scene. King Ahab of Israel and King Jehoshaphat of Judah were seated upon their thrones, and a vast crowd of people were keenly excited, for a matter of great import was about to be decided. Intent on going to war against Syria, Ahab desperately needed Judah's help; but Jehoshaphat seemed reluctant to co-operate. The enterprise was extremely hazardous, and it was not at all certain that the project was according to the mind of God. Speculation, mistrust, and doubt clouded the eyes of the royal guest. It was true that many prophets were promising victory, but they were Ahab's "yes men." The cheering crowds, the excited orators, the coaxing Ahab were unimpressive, and finally Jehoshaphat said, "Is there not here a prophet of the Lord besides, that we may enquire of him? And the king of Israel said unto Jehoshaphat, There is yet one man, by whom we may enquire of the Lord: but I hate him; for he never prophesied good unto me, but always evil: the same is Micaiah the son of Imla" (2 Chron. 18:6-8).

The Man who was Sure

"And when Micaiah was come to the king, the king said unto him, Micaiah, shall we go to Ramoth-gilead to battle, or shall I forbear?" (v. 14). And as the prophet replied, the watchful eyes of Jehoshaphat were focused upon his face. The answer was both ominous and certain, and although its delivery resulted in the preacher's imprisonment, at least the king of Judah had received his guidance. He was certain that the venture would end in disaster; that all who went forth to meet the enemy would be utterly vanquished. Ahab's chin betrayed the stubbornness of his heart, however, and the crowds encouraged his folly. The false prophets were dancing with glee. Victory seemed assured, and false enthusiasm impaired their better judgment. The cheering mobs, the shining eyes, and the shouts of excited people failed to cheer the doubtful Jehoshaphat. Everything was wrong. No battle could be won when a prophet was in prison!

The Man who was Scared

"So the king of Israel and Jehoshaphat the king of Judah went up to Ramoth-gilead. And the king of Israel said unto Jehoshaphat, I will disguise myself, and will go to the battle;

but put thou on thy robes. So the king of Israel disguised himself; and they went to the battle" (vv. 28, 29). Why did the king of Judah go to the battle when he had already ascertained that it would be unwise to do so? There can only be one answer—he was afraid. It is truly significant that this valiant warrior preferred to fight against an army than to stand against the criticisms of men. Ahab was brave and resourceful. He would go alone, and the nation would know that Jehoshaphat had turned back in an hour of danger. And Jehoshaphat trembled. Only a forthright declaration of his allegiance to God would help him. He could demand the liberation of the preacher, but would that help? Micaiah would repeat his ominous prediction. The situation demanded a *royal* prophet, but, alas, Jehoshaphat had lost his voice— and his vision—and his courage. The ancient scene reminds us that it takes far more courage to be Christian than to be a warrior on the field of battle. Sometimes tongues are sharper than swords!

The Man who was Saved

"And it came to pass, when the captains of the chariots saw Jehoshaphat, that they said, It is the king of Israel. Therefore they compassed about him to fight: but Jehoshaphat cried out, and the Lord helped him; and God moved them to depart from him. For it came to pass, that, when the captains of the chariots perceived that it was not the king of Israel, they turned back again from pursuing him." Even heathen people recognized a man who prayed, and Ahab was not of that category. Three vital thoughts are expressed in this gripping story. (i) *A great danger*. Inexcusable folly had placed the king in a position of extreme danger. Alone, and comparatively helpless, he was hemmed in by vicious heathen who would not hesitate to take his life. (ii) *A grievous distress*. "... but Jehoshaphat cried out." His prayer was heard immediately, yet it would have been better had he prayed earlier! (iii) *A glorious deliverance*. "... and the Lord helped him.... And Jehoshaphat the king of Judah returned to his house in peace to Jerusalem" (2 Chron. 19:1). Surely he was a wiser man. A fence on the top of a cliff is better than an ambulance at the bottom. It is better to pray for guidance before a calamity, than to ask for help after it.

JEHOIADA AND JOASH ... or the tale of two funerals

(2 CHRONICLES 24: 15–25)

This is the strange account of two funerals, and a more suggestive story was never told. Within six months of each other, two bodies were carried to their last earthly resting place; but casual onlookers would have been quite sure that the undertakers had ruined the funeral arrangements. In the first place, a humble priest was lifted from his unpretentious dwelling, and carried through crowded streets to be buried in the royal burial ground. "And they buried him in the city of David among the kings, because he had done good in Israel, both toward God, and toward his house (v. 16). Later that year another funeral left the royal palace, but this time the streets were empty except for a few morbid sightseers. The king had been brutally murdered, but everyone was glad. "They buried him in the city of David, but not in the sepulchres of the kings" (2 Chron. 21:20). In common with one of his predecessors, "he departed without being desired." This suggests a story, for here we have an example of the New Testament text, "The last shall be first, and the first last."

A Star Appearing

Against the sombre background of Israel's history, the coming of Joash seemed like the appearance of a new comet in the constellations of God. A strong-willed woman had ruthlessly planned the annihilation of the royal family, and only the fortitude of a brave priest had prevented the complete success of her schemings. A boy prince had been smuggled into the temple, and carefully guarded against the day of his coronation. The priest had been father, counsellor, guardian, and tutor to his young charge. "And Jehoash did that which was right in the sight of the Lord all his days wherein Jehoiada the priest instructed him. But—" (2 Kings 12:2, 3). When the faithful in Israel were beginning to despair, this dauntless prince ascended the throne of David, and immediately instituted reforms destined to transform a nation. Surely, the old priest was intensely proud of his royal scholar.

A Star Shining

"And Jehoiada made a covenant between the Lord and the king and the people, that they should be the Lord's people; between the king also and the people. And all the people of the land went into the house of Baal, and brake it down" (2 Kings 11:17, 18). And from that day a new happiness came to the hearts of Israel; the influence of the sanctuary reached every part of the nation, and the God-fearing king shone brilliantly in the national sky. Extensive repairs were carried out within the damaged temple, and the resurgence of spiritual life thrilled the heart of God. But—

A Star Slipping

It is tragic to see a wounded eagle, with its wings spread helplessly on the ground; it is even more tragic to see one of God's instruments falling into sin and shame. When the aged priest died, the king began to ignore the word of God. Then the princes made obeisance before him, and the increasing popularity turned his head. When the Lord sent messengers to warn the sinful leaders, they refused to listen. "And the Spirit of the Lord came upon Zechariah the son of Jehoiada the priest," who stood before the people and warned them of coming judgment. The king, who had once been a foster-brother to this young man, listened and secretly issued orders for his execution. "And the people conspired against Zechariah, and stoned him with stones *at the commandment of the king* in the court of the house of the Lord. Thus Joash the king remembered not the kindness which Jehoiada his father had done to him, but slew his son. And when Zechariah died, he said, The Lord look upon it, and require it."

A Star Crashing

When the new friends gathered around the king, their laughter made the utterances of the priest seem ancient and stupid. He shared their sinful gaiety. Yet it would have been better had a millstone been hanged about his neck, and he cast into the depths of the sea, rather than that he should fall into the hands of the living God. Within the brief space of six months avengers crept into the royal bedroom, and callously murdered him. The assassination probably delighted the nation. Joash had not only lost his friends, his possessions, his honour, and the respect of the nation—he had lost his soul. In the Great Assize he will be without excuse, for he had "known the Scriptures from his youth up."

UZZIAH ... and a family in decline
(2 CHRONICLES 26: 3–21)

This is the story of a quarrel in a church; it is the account of a man who did not get his own way in the conduct of the sanctuary. Such men often affirm that it is possible to be a devout worshipper without attending any church; but their statements are misleading. From time immemorial man has been his brother's keeper, and no one can persistently refrain from worshipping in the sanctuary without displeasing God and providing a bad example for other people.

The Father who Quarrelled in Church

"Sixteen years old was Uzziah when he began to reign, and he reigned fifty and two years in Jerusalem.... He did that which was right in the sight of the Lord.... He was marvellously helped, till he was strong. But when he was strong, his heart was lifted up to his destruction: for he transgressed against the Lord his God, and went into the temple of the Lord to burn incense...." This was an act of great folly, and it was not a cause for amazement when the priest followed to challenge him before the altar. The king frowned. What right had any priest to interfere with royal prerogatives? It was impertinence of the most blatant order. The meddlesome cleric should be taught a lesson.... "And while he was wroth with the priests, the leprosy even rose up in his forehead before the priests in the house of the Lord ... and, behold, he was leprous ... and they thrust him out from thence; yea, himself hasted also to go out, because the Lord had smitten him." Arrogance is always out of place before the altar of God; and anyone who would belligerently argue with the Almighty is to some degree committing suicide. "And Uzziah the king was a leper unto the day of his death, and dwelt in a several house ... and Jotham his son was over the king's house."

The Son who Stayed Away from Church

"And Jotham his son reigned in his stead ... and he did that which was right in the sight of the Lord ... *howbeit he entered not into the temple of the Lord*" (2 Chron. 26:23; 27:1, 2). Here we find a strange contrast. His grandfather, Zadok, had been a great priest (cf. 27:1), and his father also had been a believer until arrogance ruined his testimony. The new king could not conquer the bitterness of his spirit. He believed in the principles of religion; he was quite prepared to admit that they represented the greatest features in the life of the nation; but resentment lingered in his soul. His father had been punished in that temple, and his tears of repentance had been unavailing. Jotham had no wish to attend the services. He could be as good a man staying at home. King Jotham bequeathed to posterity statements that will last to the end of time. Alas, other people have quarrelled within the churches, and have followed the ancient example. They send their children to Sunday-schools, they sometimes send their offerings to maintain the church ministry; yet bitterness of heart provides a constant source of prejudice. They do not realize that the stupidity of their actions determines the attitude of their children.

The Grandson who Closed the Church

" And Jotham slept with his fathers . . . and Ahaz his son reigned in his stead. . . . He did not that which was right in the sight of the Lord . . . he made molten images for Baalim. . . . And Ahaz gathered together the vessels of the house of God, and cut in pieces the vessels of the house of God, *and shut up the doors of the house of the Lord* . . ." (2 Chron. 27:9; 28:1, 2, 24). And if great-grandfather Zadok had been able to witness this foul deed, his benign old face would have been wet with tears. It was almost inconceivable that within the span of four generations the family of a priest could so degenerate. The sacred house was sombre and silent; the huge doors were fastened, and would-be worshippers were driven away. Laughing people saw the substitute altars at the street corners, and the cause of God was ridiculed. Such was the result of the evil example given by a man who refrained from entering the house of God. Christians do well to remember the command, " Forsake not the assembling of yourselves together." The Church of Christ is the representative body of the Lord in this world. It is the divine will that all who claim allegiance to Christ should play a part in its sacred service. No man can be well-pleasing to his Lord if he persistently ignores God's wishes in regard to this important matter. In spite of the presence of hypocrites in the synagogues, Christ always attended the services. All true Christians will delight in following His example.

THE BIRDS ... which were wiser than men
(PSALM 84: 3)

I was once taken by the Baptist minister of Wellington, New South Wales, Australia, to speak at a small country church in the village of Seatonville. I had prepared well for the address to be given that afternoon, but the moment I entered the church I knew my preparation had been in vain. Since the days of my childhood, birds have been irresistible, and the beautiful nest cleverly built into the oil lamp hanging above the pulpit completely captivated my interest. The swallows had found a broken window, and had taken possession of the building. Just how they managed to weave their compact nest into the wire fittings of the lamp, I cannot tell—for that matter, can anyone tell how these things are done? The fact that services were held only occasionally in the building helped to attract the birds, and their young had been hatched amid the quiet of the sanctuary. The floor of the church was stained with evidence of their habitation, but no one seemed to care. The congregation smiled when they saw the birds, and smiled even more when the twittering friends apparently accompanied the organ music during the first hymn. I abandoned my prepared sermon, and thought of other birds which were wiser than men.

A Place of Silence

During one of David's visits to the sanctuary, he noticed that the sparrows and the swallows had also developed a liking for the sacred house. He recognized that their nests had been allowed to remain close to the altar of God, and before he returned to his palace he paused to watch them. Perhaps his own commands had something to do with the undisturbed rest enjoyed by these creatures. During the mating season the birds had flown into the sanctuary, and had perched on a beam to study their surroundings. The movements of the priests were dignified, and sound was hushed. Was not this the house of prayer? The little birds made their decision, and began to build their homes as near to the altar of God as discretion would allow. Amid the restful atmosphere the eggs were laid, and undisturbed, the birds awaited the consummation of their union. When the young first looked out of the nest they saw the altar, and quickly realized that noise was an offence in this place of peace.

A Place of Safety

They were probably frightened when the priests looked into the nest, but the custodians of the house merely smiled and walked away. Slowly but surely, fear disappeared from the minds of the feathered family. They were safe. There were no hooligans seeking to destroy or rob the nest. There were no merciless owls waiting to pounce on the young. There were no snakes creeping silently toward the defenceless family. Dangers were rare; the altar had cast a mantle of peaceful protection over the entire place. Eventually the young birds sat on the edge of their home to survey the people who drew near to the altar of God. Perhaps they even wondered why these people went away again, for surely the burning sunshine was far less comforting than the soothing shade of God's house. And so the youngsters sat and twittered among themselves; they were near to the altar; they were content.

A Place of Song

As they became older the youngsters became stronger, and their twittering developed into something more resonant. When the Levites sang the praises of God, the birds cocked their heads and appeared to listen. Eventually their songs mingled with the anthems of praise arising from other thankful hearts. King David listened to all this, and afterwards wrote, " How amiable are thy tabernacles, O Lord of hosts! My soul longeth, yea, even fainteth for the courts of the Lord ... Yea, the sparrow hath found an house, and the swallow a nest for herself, where she may lay her young, *even thine altars,* O Lord of hosts, my king, and my God. *Blessed are they that dwell in thine house: they will be still praising thee.*" There is another altar which offers sanctuary. It is a place of quiet rest; a safe place, where joy abounds in the hearts of the people of God. There, the dangers of life are offset by God's promises; the blasts of life's storms are minimized by the warmth of His love; the quality of the songs is deepened by the sense of the unfailing goodness of Christ. It is a source of endless amazement that so many people prefer to stay elsewhere. Even the birds must marvel at the stupidity of human beings.

> Said the sparrow to the swallow,
> I should really like to know
> Why these anxious human beings
> Rush about and worry so.
>
> Said the swallow to the sparrow,
> I suppose that it must be
> That they have no heavenly Father
> Such as cares for you and me.

THE GARDENER ... who neglected his weeding

(Proverbs 24: 30–34)

If King Solomon kept a diary, the pages devoted to the story of the ancient gardener made strange reading. Undoubtedly other events found space between the items of news, but when these were separated from the main story, the following was left for posterity.

April. "*I went by the field ... and by the vineyard.*" *What possibilities!*

The weather is getting warmer; spring is in the air. The trees are awakening after their long winter sleep, and all nature is beginning to sing. To-day I passed by a vineyard, and it looked lovely. The owner, a self-satisfied man, was very proud of his possession. He seemed one of the sort who never takes kindly to rebuke or instruction. He knew it all! Yet I admired his vineyard, for it presented great opportunities. It was favourably situated, well sheltered, well watered. A man could make a lot of money in that vineyard. The young vines were very healthy. I envied that dreamy husbandman. I have a haunting fear that he might neglect his picturesque garden. Ah, it was so lovely; it reminded me of a man's soul.

May. "*And lo, the vineyard was all grown over with thorns.*" *What problems!*

Yes, I was really shocked. That lovely vineyard was unrecognizable. The well-kept paths had almost disappeared; the warm brown soil was hidden. That silly man had neglected his weeding. His garden is swiftly becoming a wilderness. What a fool! I saw him on the veranda of his house. Well! His snores betrayed his whereabouts. His long legs were stretched in front of his chair, and his big hat rested on his nose! I felt like shaking him; but after all, my being king did not give me the right to interrupt a man's siesta. But he's a fool, for all that. Those weeds and thorns will increase every day, and all the possibilities so apparent last month will vanish. What would happen in my soul if I acted similarly? Weeds will grow anywhere in very quick time. The snores of that man annoyed me!

June. "*And nettles had covered the face of the vineyard.*" *What pain!*

Well, well, well! I could hardly believe my eyes. I saw that vineyard again to-day, and this time it was worse than ever! The young vines were lost in a forest of nettles. Yes, nettles, mark you! They'll take some getting out now. Somebody will be hurt before that garden is reclaimed. And would you believe it—the gardener was sleeping again. His feet were on another chair, his hat covered his face, his snores were as regular as the incoming waves of the sea. I looked at the blue skies; I felt the warmth of the glorious sunshine. It was wonderful to be alive on such a day, and yet he slept. My! Yes, it's strange how that vineyard reminds me of a human soul. A little neglect, and weeds give place to thorns; a little more neglect and thorns give place to nettles. I think the husbandman has already lost his harvest. Nettles! Weeding will be useless now. Only immediate ruthless action will save the crop!

JULY. "*And the stone wall of the vineyard was broken down.*" What peril!

Yes, I expected it! Other people have noticed the indolence of that stupid fool. He spends all his time sleeping. His vineyard is utterly neglected, and now he is being robbed. The encircling wall has been broken. I wonder who did that? Now the foxes can get in, and anyone can steal the sleeper's possessions. I had a look around the place, and soon detected evidence that thieves had been in the vineyard. I walked across to the veranda—oh, yes, he was there as usual. I was tempted to awaken him, but on second thoughts I left him. I am wondering if he will ever change his foolish habits. Anyhow, there he sat; his lower jaw was rising and falling on his heaving chest, and all the while his nasal organs produced discords! What would I have liked to do! It's not safe to write that in any diary—some day others might read my words!

AUGUST. "*Yet a little sleep . . . so shall thy poverty come.*" What poverty!

Cheers! A miracle has happened; the impossible has taken place; the dead has been resurrected. Yes, I was down there again to-day, and I could have laughed when I saw dismay written on the face of the husbandman. He had been across to witness the harvesting of the grapes in the adjacent vineyards, and was filled with remorse. He was calling himself by all the unholy names imaginable, but the nettles were higher than ever! "Then I saw, and considered it well: I looked upon it, and received instruction." Neglect can ruin any garden—even the garden of my soul. Have I been as foolish as the sleepy husbandman? I have looked at other vineyards and forgotten my own. I must get on with my own weeding. They've grown a lot lately!

FOUR MIDGETS . . . and their secret of strength

(PROVERBS 30: 24–28)

King Solomon was a very observant man, who in spite of the details of state business still found time to study the ways of Nature. He whom God had made wise, easily recognized wisdom in others; and it was this fact which led him to write, "There be four things which are little upon the earth, but they are exceeding wise: the ants . . . the conies . . . the locusts . . . the spider." Are we justified in thinking that here is a progression of thought which reminds of loftier things?

The Unsurpassed Foresight

"The ants are a people not strong, *yet they prepare their meat in the summer."* Ants love sunshine, and on a warm day these underground dwellers swarm through their tiny tunnels in search of food. When one of these creatures discovers a treasure, the news is communicated to the rest of the colony, and immediately every able-bodied creature hastens to help transport the "find" to the underground granary. When the warmth of the sunshine begins to disappear, the ants return to their home, and all through the bleak days of winter they remain hidden. The great Creator has endowed them with superlative wisdom. Recognizing their own insufficiency, they correctly assess their need and adequately prepare for the future. There are many other features about these tiny people which humans could well emulate. It is easy to understand why the Bible says, "Go to the ant, thou sluggard." Men are also in great need, and are not capable of withstanding eternal storms. It behoves them to prepare in summer—the day of opportunity—what they will need in future days.

The Unique Fortress

"The conies are but a feeble folk, *yet make they their houses in the rocks."* It is doubtful whether one could find conies anywhere except in rocks. These timid creatures have no weapons with which to fight, and therefore they seek shelter in the strongholds of nature. High on the cliffs between Capetown and Port Elizabeth in South Africa, these creatures may be seen playing in the sunshine. Yet in order to approach them, the onlooker must move slowly and quietly. The least sound is sufficient to alarm the animals, and instantly they are on the alert. A rabbit burrows into the soft earth, but the conies love rocks in the most inaccessible positions. It would be impossible to dig them out of their impregnable fortress. They seem to be wiser than men, who have more confidence in their own sufficiency than they have in the Rock of Ages.

The Undivided Fellowship

"The locusts have no king, *yet go they forth all of them by bands."* Isolated locusts present no dangers to the farmer. "United they stand: divided they fall." A swarm of locusts is something to be feared. In their millions they appear on the horizon, and their passing suggests the drone of a great aeroplane. In Central Africa and elsewhere in the world these innumerable pests sometimes obliterate the sun. Their coming represents a major disaster, and vast sums of money are spent annually in the attempt to annihilate this menace. The locusts have no leader, but as long as they stay together they represent a striking force which makes men fear. Alas, they might be our school masters. The fellowship of saints should be the greatest thing in the world. The Bible speaks of the one-ness of the Body of Christ, but in actual experience assemblies and individuals isolate themselves from other Christians. They divide the family of God, and substitute impotence for power. All true Christians value the fellowship of other believers. Real saints are never hermits nor spiritual tramps!

The Undaunted Fortitude

"The spider taketh hold with her hands, *and is in king's palaces."* Obviously King Solomon knew this to be true. Probably he had often destroyed a spider's web, only to find that another soon appeared in its place. The spider's motto seems to be, "If at first you don't succeed, try, try again." This courageous spirit has been invincible during the ages. The very existence of the spider depends upon its ability to overcome persecution. Its magnificent fortitude has conquered kingdoms. No military guard can subjugate it, and even the greatest watchfulness is not a guarantee against the spider's coming. The hunted creature takes hold anywhere in order to weave a web. We are reminded of the words of Christ: "No man, having put his hand to the plough, and looking back, is fit for the kingdom of God." These ancient midgets can teach all who are not too old to learn.

MR. INSIGNIFICANCE . . . who should have been knighted
(ECCLESIASTES 9: 14, 15)

Dear Sir,
Don't laugh, but we have found you a wife! You are astonished; of course, we expected you to be, but you must blame King Solomon. We never had the privilege of meeting you face to face, but your famous exploit has been handed down through history, and Solomon's admiration has spread to other hearts. Again and again we have read the words, "There was a little city and few men within it; and there came a great king against it, and besieged it, and built great bulwarks against it: Now there was found in it a poor wise man, and he by his wisdom delivered the city; yet no man remembered that same poor man." We didn't like the forgetfulness of your fellow-citizens; but there, let us return to the point which matters—we have found you a wife. Did you ever hear of the wise woman who saved her city? She belonged to your generation, and her intervention prevented the death of her fellow-citizens. Solomon knew all about her, for it was his father's army which threatened to destroy her home. What is the matter, little wise man? You are laughing! Good gracious! You have good reason to know her! Surely, friend, she isn't your wife already? Now we are guessing, and shall always wonder if that city was saved by your joint efforts.

How Feeble

We remember that when David returned after his flight from Absalom, his homecoming was marred by the insurrection of a man named Sheba. General Joab pursued through the nation, and finally overtook him at the city of Abel in Beth-maachah. It is recorded that ". . . they cast up a bank against the city, and it stood in the trench: and all the people that were with Joab battered the wall, to throw it down. Then cried a wise woman out of the city, Hear, hear; say, I pray you, unto Joab, Come near hither, that I may speak with thee. . . . Then she spake saying . . . I am one of them that are peaceable and faithful in Israel: thou seekest to destroy a city and a mother in Israel: why wilt thou swallow up the inheritance of the Lord?" (2 Samuel 20: 15-19). Now little wise man, we read Solomon's words concerning your home, "There was a little city, and few men within it, and there came a great king against it, and besieged it, and built great bulwarks against it." The parallel is obvious. Both places were small, and in great danger. The great king was undoubtedly David, whose men were being led by Joab. Oh, wise man, why didn't Solomon write more?

How Fortunate

"Then the woman went unto the people in her wisdom," and her advice prevented immeasurable disaster. "Now there was found in the city a poor wise man, and he by his wisdom delivered the city." Friend, we want to ask all kinds of questions. Solomon would have been conversant with the happenings of his time, and every man in Joab's army knew of the woman who foiled the determined attempt to batter the city into submission. Her wisdom would have appealed to Prince Solomon, and we wonder if he went forth in search of the heroine. Little wise man, did he discover that she was your wife; that she only put into operation the plans which you conceived? Your psychology was excellent. The invader would be more lenient when dealing with a woman! Anyhow, your fellow-citizens should have been exceedingly grateful. It would have been tragic had you been away on holiday—wouldn't it?

How Forgetful

Friend, you should have been knighted! A deputation from the highest authority should have proceeded to your home, to offer you the greatest reward possible. But that never happened. Were you disappointed, Mr. Insignificance? The people stood about in groups discussing the exciting events of the day, but none called to say "Thank you." You were poor! They could have helped a great deal, but they took things for granted and left you alone. Did you sit and discuss the matters with your wife? Did she look through the window, expecting to see someone approaching? Was she a little weary when the days passed by and you were forgotten? You were destined to enjoy the most excellent company. There was Another who became poor, in order to save many cities. He succeeded at great cost. His precious blood bought redemption for sinners; His intercession prevented untold tragedy. Yet, in return, the people despised and rejected Him. The people who owed most to Him, were the first to forget Him. You and He would have much in common. Indeed, old friend, it was worth losing your knighthood to secure His fellowship.

THE APOTHECARY ... who had flies in his ointment
(ECCLESIASTES 10: 1)

King Solomon was a very observant man. This fact is proved by the great number of object lessons mentioned in his writings. His parables and proverbs were based almost exclusively upon the happenings of everyday life, and sometimes the wise man had the ability to see the sublime in the ridiculous. His statement concerning "the flies in the ointment" has become famous, and belongs to every man's vocabulary. When the king heard of the event in the shop of the royal perfumer he probably smiled, but even he could not have guessed that his musings on the matter were to become internationally famous in all ages. The needs of the palace made great demands upon the apothecaries, for Solomon delighted in an abundance of female companions!

The Ointment Unspoiled

The supplier was very pleased with himself. He had spent much time on the preparation, and now he was satisfied. This was a present fit for the king. Its aroma was captivating and irresistible; its fragrance superseded anything previously known. The quivering nostrils and shining eyes of all his friends told him that he had succeeded at last. He had perfected fragrance. He paused to enjoy his triumph; possibly he sat down and became reminiscent of all the efforts which led to this supreme achievement. Was he called away unexpectedly? Did some other external problem precipitate itself into the mind of the satisfied apothecary? Surely something of the sort happened, for no fly could get into the ointment unless the lid had been left off the box.

The Ointment Unguarded

In a land where flies were, and still are, bred by the million; where the winged nuisances succeed in annoying everybody, it would not be long before these "flies of death" were attracted to the box of loveliness. Their spidery legs would venture on the spongy sea of colour; their twitching heads would revel in the attracting aromas; their wings would drag in the clinging mass. This was a dreadful anti-climax; the ruination of a king's delight. Why didn't that stupid man put the lid on the box? He should have known that enemies abound in this world; and that all presents for royalty must be well guarded.

The Ointment Unexamined

Now, we could forgive the perfumer if an unexpected call interfered with his work; if some momentary forgetfulness intervened. But, alas, we cannot forgive the inexcusable. A fly going into the ointment is not sufficient to make it stink! And if the word seems unpleasant, blame Solomon, for after all, it was the word he used. No ointment can deteriorate instantaneously. If the ointment be revolting, then *the flies were permitted to stay in the ointment.* The satisfied apothecary did not come back to examine his precious concoction until the dead flies had ruined it. Had they been extracted from the imprisoning substances, the perfume would have retained its bewitching qualities. Alas, this was not done, and fragrance was superseded by foulness. Probably this kind of thing had happened before; it has certainly happened since. Dead flies can spoil any ointment.

The Ointment Unattractive

What a shame! That illustrious box might have graced the boudoir of the Queen of Sheba. Its contents might easily have enhanced the charm of Pharaoh's daughter. Its irresistible power might have secured immortal fame for the man whose ingenuity brought it into being. Instead, it found a place in the refuse bin, and the apothecary had to begin all over again. Mr. Perfumer, why didn't you put the lid on the box? Yes, we know what you are thinking—why don't we do likewise when our best gifts are ready for the King of kings? Ananias and Sapphira had a rare gift, but they went away to sell a house when they might have been killing flies. David, Judas, Demas, also suffered grievous loss because flies ruined their ointment.

The Ointment Unsurpassed

"Then took Mary a pound of ointment of spikenard, very costly, and anointed the feet of Jesus, and wiped His feet with her hair: and the house was filled with the odour of the ointment" (John 12:3). Obviously Solomon's apothecary tried again, and his noble art was handed down through the generations until finally the product of his trade was produced somewhere within reach of Bethany. We do not know how Mary obtained her treasure; we only know she was careful to keep the lid on the box. She did this with all her lovely perfumes. Yet every time the Lord drew near, she hastened to display her treasures, and the world was enriched by her deeds. A Ministry of Health notice gives the command, "Swat that fly." It's not a bad idea! Flies and perfume are not ideal companions.

THE CHURCH . . . as she ought to be
(Song of Solomon 6: 10)

The Song of Solomon presents a charming study of the virtues and problems of Abishag the Shulamite. Loved by her shepherd boy, and wooed by King Solomon, she was obliged to choose between her suitors. (See *Bible Cameos,* p. 75.) This fascinating story illustrates the greater truths of the New Testament, and it is not difficult to recognize a portrait of the Church—the Bride of the Good Shepherd. Solomon's description of the most charming woman in Israel is exceedingly picturesque. Many Bible teachers declare that God was supplying therein details concerning the fulfilment of His purposes in Christ. To say the least, readers will be stimulated by the royal description of the charms of the Shulamite. "Who is she that looketh forth as the morning, fair as the moon, clear as the sun, and terrible as an army with banners?"

The Church Rejoicing

"Who is she that looketh forth as the morning. . . ? " The picture of a fair woman standing on the threshold of her home to survey the glory of the rising sun, is most enchanting. The sunlight glistens on her hair, and her countenance is as fresh as the morning dew; she smiles and hails the new day, for the darkness of the night has vanished. The sun has risen in splendour, and the gloom has disappeared. Her heart and lips re-echo the songs of the waking birds. We are reminded of Paul's injunction to the Church. He commanded them to rejoice " and make melody in their hearts " (Ephes. 5: 19). The darkness of the night of sin had ended. The tragedy of the cross had been eclipsed. The Church now heralded the dawn of a new day. Her soul vibrated; her songs arose to the throne of God. It was morning; the night had gone!

The Church Reflecting

"Who is she . . . fair as the moon. . . ? " The moon has no light of its own; it is content to reflect the light of the sun. An arc of attractive beauty, it absorbs more and more of the sun's radiance until, filled with luminant charm, it reigns supreme in the night sky. Mariners look to it, and are glad; travellers smile into its face, and feel less lonely. The moon shines resplendently because it catches the light of the sun and transmits it to a darkened world. There could hardly be a more suitable picture of the vocation and privilege of the Christian Church. We have no light of ourselves. We look to Him and are lightened. Then, having received light from the Light of the World, it is our duty to let our light shine before men, that they may see our good works and glorify our Father who is in heaven. The shining light of the Church has enabled mariners in all ages to set a course for the shelter of God's harbour.

The Church Radiant

"Who is she . . . clear as the sun. . . ?" The sun is an orb of unparalleled brilliance; the giver of life and light to the world. Without its glorious ministry, men would linger in darkness. When the sun arises in eastern splendour, the birds begin to sing; and when it sinks in western skies, they hush their songs and go to sleep. The world grows weary when the sun has gone, and hopes it will soon return to bring a fine day to-morrow. It is the sun which attracts moisture, and then allows it to fall in gentle showers upon a thirsty land. It is the sun which warms the earth, turning it into the caress of a mother—a mother who brings her children to birth, and then feeds them until they are ready to meet the demands of the waiting world. Radiance unlimited—service unending—glory unprecedented. These are God's descriptions of His Church—as He meant her to be.

The Church Reclaiming

"Who is she . . . terrible as an army with banners?" Even Solomon recognized the irresistible charm of this gracious woman. She was most desirable; she was invincible, for against her winsomeness and beauty no man could stand. She captured the strongest; she reduced her greatest critics to impotence; she was an army marching to victory—an army whose waving banners struck fear to the breasts of opponents. Perhaps the New Testament authors had this picture in mind when they recorded the statements of the enemies of the Church who said, "They who have turned the world upside down are come here also." Reclaiming lost territory for Christ, the ransomed of the Lord went from strength to strength—terrible as an army with banners.

We see God's portrait of the Church; but let us pause a moment to consider. Surely something is wrong. Either God is a poor artist, or His model has changed. I wonder which it could be?

ISAIAH... who loved drawing water out of wells
(ISAIAH 12: 3)

Not many men are capable of expressing much in little, and more often than not inflation turns little into much. Isaiah was one of those remarkable men whom God enabled to express the whole range of truth within the astonishingly small compass of six verses. His message primarily refers to the future glory of Israel, but the truth expressed therein may be found in any act of God's saving grace. These thrilling facts are as evident in Israel's exodus from Egypt, and a sinner's deliverance from sin, as in the future reconciliation of the Jewish people. Let us consider the three divisions clearly outlined by the prophet.

God My Salvation—a great pardon

"And in that day thou shalt say, O Lord ... though thou wast angry with me, thine anger is turned away, and thou comfortest me. Behold, God is my salvation; I will trust, and not be afraid" (vv. 1-2). Isaiah's opening statement limits the scope and fulfilment of the promise. This glad experience belongs to a certain day when necessary conditions are forthcoming. It is the day of Christ's coronation, when people bow at His feet to acclaim His royalty. When Christ is enthroned in human affection, God mercifully dispenses forgiveness, and "in that day" men and women are able to say, "though thou wast angry with me, thine anger is turned away, and thou comfortest me." Three stimulating words seem to be evident in this theme. (i) *Compassion.* God's mercy has been revealed to man. The sin which caused divine wrath has been put away. (ii) *Conversion.* The sinner has turned from his sin, to accept and kneel before the Lord. Rebellion has given place to redemption. (iii) *Comfort.* The forgiven heart has now become the home of peace. Soothing comfort has banished worry, and the peace of God which passeth understanding now floods the soul.

God My Strength—a great provision

"... for the Lord Jehovah is my strength ... therefore with joy shall ye draw water out of the wells of salvation.... Cry out and shout, thou inhabitant of Zion: for great is the Holy One of Israel in the midst of thee" (vv. 2-6). The challenge of the new life makes men tremble, for they fear inherent weakness. The prophet points out that the strength of the redeemed is in the Redeemer. The God who saves is the God who strengthens. The ransomed of the Lord are not left to wander alone along the paths of life. "The Holy One of Israel is in the midst of thee." This wonderful truth was clearly illustrated by the presence of the ark of the covenant in the midst of Israel. In all the wilderness journeys the sacred emblem of God's presence accompanied the tribes, and unless sin offended God, its presence guaranteed divine favour. God never left His people alone. God valued fellowship, and came down to tabernacle among men. It is this sublime fact which deepens desire, and strengthens arms to " draw water from the wells of God's salvation." We do well to remember that God's bounty is in wells. The first taste of living water does not exhaust the supply. Conversion is but the glorious introduction to the inexhaustible riches of Christ. Nevertheless, water does not run automatically from wells. Someone with intense desire must draw it forth. God's provision does not minimize human responsibility. God supplies strength, but I must use my arms.

God My Song—a great peace

" . . . the Lord Jehovah is my strength and my song. . . . Therefore with *joy* shall ye draw water out of the wells of salvation. And in that day shall ye say, Praise the Lord . . ." (vv. 2-4). *"In that day."* Joy naturally follows when people walk with God. Forgiveness, fellowship, fearlessness, contribute their quota to the enrichment of all who have acclaimed and accepted the King. Sorrow and sighing disappear, and deep content fills the soul. Three additional words seem to appear on Isaiah's manuscript. (i) *Confidence.* God's wells never run dry ; the Lord in the midst of His people, will never leave His redeemed children. (ii) *Courage.* This is good news which should be told to all nations. The eyes of the saints are turned toward other people, and a desire to witness springs in the heart. (iii) *Confession.* " . . . declare his doings among the people, make mention that his name is exalted. Sing unto the Lord ; for he hath done excellent things: this is known in all the earth " (vv. 4-5). Isaiah put down his pen. His remarkable chapter abruptly ended, as though he had lost his inspiration. Probably he was busy with a new job—drawing water out of a well!

ISAIAH . . . who saw God's love in disguise
(Isaiah 30: 15–26)

It has often been said that affliction is the Good Shepherd's black dog. When God's people wander from the fold of the Great Shepherd and stubbornly refuse to return, God permits affliction to act as a sheepdog. It would appear that this statement is based upon fact, for oftentimes trouble has begotten blessing in the hearts of men when prosperity only increased indifference to spiritual realities.

God's Love Disguised

"For thus saith the Lord God, the Holy One of Israel; In returning and rest shall ye be saved; in quietness and in confidence shall be your strength: *and ye would not.* But ye said, No; for we will flee upon horses. . . . And though the Lord give you the bread of adversity, and the water of affliction . . ." (vv. 15-20). It is a stimulating thought that God's love always outlives man's rebellion. It is also a cause for eternal thanksgiving that, although His methods of dealing with sinful man may change from time to time, God never abandons His children. The grapes of Eshcol may be superseded by the bread of adversity, and the glittering joys of triumph may be temporarily overwhelmed by the waters of affliction; but through all the changing scenes of life, God's unfailing love safeguards His people. He makes all things work together for their good, until "the people shall dwell in Zion . . . and shall weep no more" (v. 19).

God's Love Displayed

". . . yet shall not thy teachers be removed into a corner any more, but thine eyes shall see thy teachers" (v. 20). There is always hope for a nation which possesses a prophet! A man's outlook can never be completely dark when he holds an open Bible! The very fact that God desires to speak with sinners is evidence that He wants to win them. If the Lord had abandoned the nation, He would have ceased sending His messengers. In spite of the disguise, God's love was still visible. The prophet was thrilled when he was able to say, "He will be very gracious unto thee at the voice of thy cry; when he shall hear it, he will answer thee" (v. 19).

God's Love Disturbing

"And thine ears shall hear a word behind thee, saying, This is the way, walk ye in it, when ye turn to the right hand,

and when ye turn to the left" (v. 21). The road of correction may be very grievous, but the Lord is never far away. His eyes watch, and His care plans, and whenever sinful man begins to flounder in uncertainty, a still small voice whispers, "This is the way, walk ye in it." Turn around, O silly one. Don't you know that I am *helping* you? Can't you hear that I am calling you? Turn around, O backsliding Israel, and I will heal thy backslidings. "This is the way, walk ye in it." An interesting parallel is found in the first chapter of Revelation. The great phases of John's spiritual experience are clearly outlined. (i) "I heard *behind* me a great voice" (Rev. 1:10). (ii) "And I turned to see the voice that spake with me" (1:12). (iii) "And being turned, I saw . . . one like unto the Son of man" (vv. 12, 13). (iv) "And when I saw him, I fell at his feet" (v. 17). God is never too busy to seek His wandering children.

God's Love Delivered

"Moreover the light of the moon shall be as the light of the sun, and the light of the sun shall be seven-fold, as the light of seven days, in the day that the Lord bindeth up the breach of his people, and healeth the stroke of their wound" (Isa. 30:26). Many competent teachers declare that this ancient prophecy has still to be fulfilled. They assert that it can never be completely realized until the Lord Jesus returns to set up His earthly kingdom. Probably their claim would stand the test of enquiry, nevertheless we need not wait until that glad day before we discover proof of the accuracy of these words. They are being fulfilled every day in the experience of multitudes of people. Wanderers are even now hearing the whispers of God's Spirit, and those who are tired of straying are already turning in response to the call of God. The "*and ye would not*" of Isaiah 30:15 refers to a people who turned before it was too late. A similar statement is found in Matthew 23:37. Alas, it refers to people who had no desire to turn.

A stitch in time saves nine; a turn in time saves eternity!

ISAIAH ... and his broken pen
(ISAIAH 42: 1-3; MATTHEW 12: 14-21)

It would appear that a delightful word-picture may be found in this text. The prophet had been gathering the thin reeds which grew so plentifully in the Jordan valley. Tied in a neat bundle, they were now attached to his belt, as he sat at his writing table. The end of the reeds had been sharpened, and with ink close at hand, the scribe commenced to write. When the reed point became too saturated, Isaiah discarded his pen, lifted another reed from the bundle at his side, and the work continued. Then suddenly the writer frowned. His new quill had been damaged. Somehow it had been bruised, and as he exerted pressure upon it, the reed buckled within his fingers. He was about to throw it down when suddenly a whisper thrilled his soul. "When Messiah comes, a bruised reed shall he not break, and the smoking flax shall he not quench...." Seven centuries later Matthew remembered the prophet's statement, and because he could find no more suitable words to express his feelings, he cited Isaiah's prediction in his gospel.

The Lord's Great Patience

Isaiah saw broken reeds; Christ saw broken men; Matthew saw reeds and men, and they were strangely alike. Even the best of us are apt to be unreliable at times, and it would seem then that all God's labour has been in vain. When He would take and use us for the fulfilment of His will, flaws make us unfit for service. We are not as He had hoped; sin has ruined our spiritual dependability. Why did Matthew think of this text at that particular moment? "Then the Pharisees went out, and held a council against him, how they might destroy him. But when Jesus knew it, he withdrew himself from thence: and great multitudes followed him, *and he healed them all*" (Matt. 12:14-15). He knew no bitterness of spirit, and discrimination was unknown in His actions. He healed them *all*. Even the disappointing human reeds received their share of blessing, for He refused to discard them. Why was this so?

The Lord's Great Purpose

Did Isaiah correctly anticipate the question which would arise in the minds of all his readers? Why should the Lord patiently persevere with broken reeds, when so many others were within reach? The prophet smiled and changed his simile: "And the smoking flax shall he not quench...." We see the smouldering flax and the thin wisp of smoke lazily curling upward from its black edge. A brilliant flame once burned there, but something has interfered with the flow of fuel; the glow has disappeared; the light has gone. Impetuosity says, "Pinch it out." Hope replies, "No. Gently breathe upon it, and do all that is possible to renew the flame. When Messiah comes, ' the smoking flax shall he not quench.' " There are men within whose hearts the fires of God once burned, but alas, hindrances prevented the continuance of their usefulness. Their flame of devotion faltered, dwindled, and ultimately disappeared. They who once shone brightly for God have now backslidden into the shadows. Faint wisps of smoke tell their own sorry tale of spiritual depression and frustration—of a soul which is like a piece of smoking flax. Law demands judgment; but grace refuses, and proceeds to try and rekindle the flame within the human heart.

The Lord's Great Praise

"And in his name shall the Gentiles trust." Matthew watched the surging crowds, and knew that no man was denied access to Christ. Jew and Gentile, rich and poor; all were welcomed and all were healed. And in one glorious burst of revelation, the disciple recognized the purpose of God in Christ. He had come to seek and to save that which was lost; and through His power even the most degraded men, the most unresponsive and sinful of men, could be lifted to higher realms of spiritual experience. The kingdom of God could never be limited by racial barriers, and Jewish prejudice could never prevent the outflow of divine love. All men had a place in the affections of the Highest—" till he send forth judgment unto victory," or as one has said, " till judgment be overcome by victory." Seven centuries divided the two scribes. Isaiah looked on; Matthew looked back; and their vision met in Christ. A broken pen! A broken man! Isaiah thought of his reed; Matthew thought of himself; and probably both were glad to say, " And in his name . . . shall we all trust."

> How sweet the name of Jesus sounds
> In a believer's ear:
> It soothes his sorrows, heals his wounds,
> And drives away his fear

ISAIAH ... the man with the telescopic sight
(ISAIAH 53)

The fifty-third chapter of Isaiah represents the greatest prophetic utterance of Old Testament literature. It is a thrilling fact that a man who lived seven centuries before the incarnation saw clearly the details of the death of Christ. Isaiah had telescopic eyes which penetrated seven centuries of the unrevealed.

Isaiah saw the death of Christ, and understood its purpose

" . . . and the Lord hath laid on him the iniquity of us all . . . he was cut off out of the land of the living: for the transgression of my people was *the stroke upon him* " (vv. 6-8). This was contrary to most of the Messianic predictions, which foretold an earthly kingdom of abiding splendour. Nevertheless it harmonized with the types and shadows of Old Testament teaching, where God declared that " without the shedding of blood there is no remission." Christ sought a kingdom—a kingdom within the cleansed hearts of His people. He died to put away their sin.

Isaiah saw Christ's burial in the tomb of Joseph of Arimathea

" And he made his grave with the wicked, *and with the rich in his death* " (v. 9). Although Christ would die the death of a malefactor, His body would not be interred in a common grave. " When the even was come, there came a rich man.... He went to Pilate, and begged the body of Jesus. ... And laid it in his own new tomb, which he had hewn out of the rock " (Matt. 27:57-60).

Isaiah saw the conversion of the thief

"... when thou shalt make his soul an offering for sin, he shall see his seed . . . " (v. 10). This was a most remarkable utterance. Man's part in the crucifixion was only a means to an end. " It pleased the Lord to bruise him." Yet at the very moment when the Christ would be offered for sin, He would see His seed—His first child. We need hardly be reminded that even though the two thieves cursed the Lord Jesus, one eventually sought and found forgiveness.

Isaiah saw the resurrection of Christ

" . . . he shall prolong his days " (v. 10). At the time of Isaiah's prophecy it seemed fantastic that anyone to be so brutally put to death should be able to continue His ministry.

Surely death would terminate effort. The prophet merely shook his head and declared that the grave would be conquered. The rich man's tomb would be unable to retain its body.

Isaiah saw the prosperity of the cause of Christ

". . . and the pleasure of the Lord shall prosper in his hand. He shall see of the travail of his soul, and shall be satisfied" (vv. 10, 11). Travail is a term extensively used in connection with child-birth. Did the prophet know that through the sacrificial death of Christ, living souls would be born again into the family of God? ". . . by his knowledge shall my righteous servant justify *many*; for he shall bear their iniquities." The conversion of the thief would only be the prelude to a great symphony of praise arising from the hearts of the redeemed host.

Isaiah saw that Christ would be accompanied by two thieves

". . . and he was numbered with the transgressors" (v. 12). This might mean that in the sight of God, Christ was numbered among the sons of men; that as the representative of a guilty race, He would reconcile us to God. Yet it appears more likely that the prophet's eyes had detected the presence of another thief, and that Christ in their midst signified He was numbered among transgressors.

Isaiah heard Christ's prayer for a guilty people

". . . he made intercession for the transgressors" (v. 12). "Then said Jesus, Father, forgive them; for they know not what they do" (Luke 23:34). Are we justified in suggesting that Isaiah's vision saw another great fact—that Christ as the high priest of His people would intercede before the throne of God?

Isaiah saw the exaltation of Christ

"Therefore will I divide him a portion with the great, and he shall divide the spoil with the strong" (v. 12). The cross led to the coronation; the crucified became the conqueror. Isaiah had great eyes! He was also a great preacher! Excellent vision and effective preaching are born at Calvary.

EZEKIEL . . . and his sermon about three great men

(EZEKIEL 14: 14)

Ezekiel was interested ; the elders of Israel were approaching to seek an audience with the prophet of God. Calmly he stood to welcome them ; he bade them be seated, but before he could enquire concerning the purpose of their visit his spirit stirred within him, and a voice whispered, " Son of man, these men have set up their idols in their heart, and put the stumbling block of their iniquity before their face: should I be enquired of at all by them?" (14:3). The elders were a little dumbfounded when Ezekiel commenced to preach. His condemnation of Israel, and his comments concerning Jerusalem, were terrible. And when he finally said, " Though these three men, Noah, Daniel, and Job, were in it, they should deliver but their own souls by their righteousness, saith the Lord," the picture seemed blacker than ever.

A Man Great in Preaching

" Though Noah were in it . . . he should deliver but his own soul." The elders of Israel instantly thought of their sacred records. The sin of the antediluvian world had been so abominable that God had been obliged to send judgment. Noah, a faithful preacher, had witnessed of God's righteousness ; but his message had been rejected. Yet the Lord had been very gracious, for Noah had been the means of saving his family. Eight souls had been preserved within the ark, and the human race had not perished entirely. Yet now God declared that even were Noah present in this sinful land, he would be unable to save any other person. " Though these three men were in it, as I live, saith the Lord, they shall deliver neither sons nor daughters, but they only shall be delivered themselves " (v. 18).

A Man Great in Prayer

" Though Daniel were in it . . . he should deliver but his own soul." Daniel was a man of prayer . . . a friend of God, and the greatest figure in the nation. In spite of persecutors, this fearless man deliberately opened his windows and prayed with his face toward Jerusalem. At other times, when the wise men of Babylon were threatened with annihilation, this same Daniel sought an audience with God, and discovered all he wished to know. He was a man of the same calibre as Abraham, who knew how to prevail with God. The elders of Israel remembered how the patriarch had interceded for

Sodom, and how, although he ultimately failed to save the city, at least his intercession delivered Lot and his two daughters. While the elders considered these things, Ezekiel repeated his former statement, "Though Noah, Daniel, and Job, were in it, as I live, saith the Lord, they shall deliver neither sons nor daughters, but they only shall be delivered themselves."

A Man Great in Patience

"Though Job were in it . . . he should deliver but his own soul." This was the prophet's greatest statement, for Job stood alone in splendid magnificence. The Lord had said concerning him, "Hast thou considered my servant Job, that *there is none like him in the earth,* a perfect and an upright man, one that feareth God, and escheweth evil" (Job 1:8). The account of Job's steadfastness under trial, and of his subsequent triumph when God abundantly rewarded him for his faithfulness, was known to all Israel. Job was the man who could stand against any force of evil. Ezekiel shook his head and answered, " No." If these three saints had been transformed into one super man—if Noah had continually preached; if the prayers of Daniel had been added to Noah's preaching; and if this mighty effort had been sustained by the patience of Job—" Though these three men were in it . . . they shall deliver neither sons nor daughters, but they only shall be delivered themselves." Probably the elders were despondent as they heard these words; their case was hopeless!

A God Great in Pity

The end of Ezekiel's message was astonishing; the preacher suddenly introduced a new note to his theme. An unmistakable tenderness shone in his eyes, as he said, " Thus saith the Lord God. . . . Yet, behold, therein shall be left a remnant that shall be brought forth, both sons and daughters: behold, they shall come forth unto you, and ye shall see their way and their doings: and ye shall be comforted . . . and ye shall know that I have not done without cause all that I have done in it, saith the Lord God " (vv. 21-23). Though Noah, Daniel, and Job were present, they would not be able to rescue one son nor one daughter. Yet, God would rescue both sons and daughters. God's grace is always greater than man's sin, " For as the heaven is high above the earth, so great is his mercy . . . " (Psa. 103:11).

> O Love of God, how strong, how true:
> Eternal, and yet ever new.

HAGGAI ... the prophet with a punch
(HAGGAI 1: 6)

The minor prophets were men who believed in short sermons; they did not waste words. Undoubtedly they were raised up to meet specific needs. They were called of God to minister at a certain time in a certain way, and once their task was performed they disappeared from the scene. Haggai was one of these men, and we cannot read his message without wishing there were more of it. His words were vital, gripping, and sometimes scathing. He knew how to preach; he was a prophet with a punch! His appearance was most providential, for the city of God was in ruins. Selfishness dominated the hearts of the nation; and as long as the people enjoyed the comfort of their own homes, the temple was forgotten.

A Bag with Holes

"Then came the word of the Lord by Haggai the prophet, saying, Is it time for you, O ye, to dwell in your ceiled houses, and this house lie waste? Now, therefore, thus saith the Lord of hosts; Consider your ways. Ye have sown much, and bring in little; ye eat, but ye have not enough; ye drink, but ye are not filled with drink; ye clothe you, but there is none warm; and *he that earneth wages earneth wages to put it into a bag with holes*. . . . Consider your ways" (1:3-7). It would not be difficult to imagine the prophet giving Israel an object lesson with an old bag. His coins fell to the ground, and the folly of his action increased the effectiveness of his preaching. And after each forceful point in his message, the prophet pointed to the wrecked house of God. No man can be truly prosperous when His sanctuary is neglected. No person can be supremely happy when the music of his soul is silent. Haggai continued, "Who is left among you that saw this house in her first glory? and how do ye see it now? is it not in your eyes in comparison of it as nothing" (2:3). The prophet's questions reached the hearts of the hearers, and the people were humbled before God.

A Building with Holiness

Within seven weeks (Haggai 1:1—2:1) the Spirit of the Lord completely changed the outlook of the self-satisfied nation, and the prophet was able to encourage the repentant people. "The silver is mine, and the gold is mine, saith the Lord of hosts. The glory of this latter house shall be greater than of the former, saith the Lord of hosts; and in this place will I give peace ..." (2:8, 9). And as the work of reconstruction proceeded, the prophet watched and waited, and finally, " In the four and twentieth day of the ninth month, in the second year of Darius, came the word of the Lord by Haggai the prophet, saying, Thus saith the Lord of hosts; Ask now the priests concerning the law . . . " (2:10, 11). This inspired speaker excelled in the noble art of painting word pictures. His bag with holes was followed by his building of holiness. He had very definite ideas concerning the path to prosperity and happiness. God's hand had been against His people because their sin had offended Him. He said, " I smote you with blasting and with mildew and with hail in all the labours of your hands ; yet ye turned not to me, said the Lord " (2:17). " Whom the Lord loveth he chasteneth," and this fact had been very evident in the divine dealings with Israel. Haggai seemed to be saying, " Seek ye first the kingdom of God, and his righteousness ; and all these things shall be added unto you " (Matt. 6:33).

A Benediction with Hope

" Consider now from this day and upward . . . from the day that the foundation of the Lord's house was laid, consider it . . . from this day will I bless you " (2:18, 19). The promises given to Israel were far-reaching and assuring. No weapon formed against them should prosper. God would destroy the kingdoms of the heathen, and overthrow every opponent of Israel. The sanctuary should be the guiding star in Israel's destiny, and beneath its shadow, every man should dwell safely. " In that day, saith the Lord of hosts, will I take thee, O Zerubbabel, my servant . . . and will make thee as a signet: for I have chosen thee, saith the Lord " (2:22, 23). Thus would the holes be repaired in the bag of Israel's fortunes ; thus would happiness return to the hearts of the people. Haggai was a man with a message. He knew how to hit hard—very hard. He knew also how to encourage repentant souls, and lead them to greater heights of spiritual endeavour. What was the secret of his success? " . . . the word of the Lord came to him." Haggai never preached until he was certain of his message. He lit his torch at the altar of God, and went forth as a flame of fire. Alas, others were like glow-worms—their lights disappeared in face of danger.

ZECHARIAH . . . and his comprehensive picture of the Gospel

(ZECHARIAH 3: 1-8)

Zechariah looked into heaven, and the story of his vision is recorded in the third chapter of his prophetic writings. "And he shewed me Joshua the high priest standing before the angel of the Lord, and Satan standing at his right hand to resist him. And the Lord said unto Satan, The Lord rebuke thee, O Satan; even the Lord that hath chosen Jerusalem rebuke thee: is not this a brand plucked out of the fire?" This is a wonderful picture of the inexhaustible riches of grace.

Joshua Cleansed

"Now Joshua was clothed with filthy garments, and stood before the angel. And he answered and spake unto those who stood before him, saying, Take away the filthy garments from him. And unto him he said, Behold, I have caused thine iniquity to pass from thee." No sin could be permitted to remain in the presence of God; thus cleansing was the first requirement of the sinner. The very stain of sin had to be removed before man could enjoy fellowship with God. Every Israelite was commanded to take an offering to the priest; and it was a basic feature in Israel's theology that apart from sacrifice, pardon was unprocurable. John the Baptist indicated that these types were fulfilled in Christ; that He would be the Lamb of God to take away the sins of the world. Thus God in Christ would be able to say to a vast host of people, "Behold, I have caused thine iniquity to pass from thee."

Joshua Clothed

"And I will clothe thee with a change of raiment." The angel of the Lord stood by as the dilapidated clothing was removed from the willing priest; he smiled as the new garments were accepted by the wondering man. He was gratified indeed when the once shabby Joshua stood resplendent and ready for his dignified office. A similar scene was witnessed in Eden when God removed the unsatisfactory clothing made by Eve, and provided new garments of salvation. Another illustration may be found in the Gospels, for when the people of Gadara came out to see what had transpired among the swineherds, "they found the man, out of whom the devils were departed, sitting at the feet of Jesus, *clothed,* and in his right mind" (Luke 8:35). Probably Christ had presented the garments to a man, who was now overjoyed and willing to accept them. To Joshua and many others the Lord says, "I will clothe thee with change of raiment."

Joshua Crowned

"And I said, Let them set a fair mitre upon his head. So they set a fair mitre upon his head, and clothed him with garments. And the angel of the Lord stood by." The mitre suggests priesthood; the mitre set on the head suggests a crown—a royal priesthood. We are reminded of the song of the redeemed in heaven: "And they sung a new song, saying, Thou art worthy ... for thou wast slain, and hast redeemed us to God by thy blood out of every kindred, and tongue, and people, and nation; and hast made us unto our God *kings and priests*"—a kingdom of priests (Rev. 5:9, 10). Had Paul the same thought in mind when he wrote, "... God, who is rich in mercy, for his great love wherewith he loved us, even when we were dead in sins, hath quickened us together with Christ ... and hath raised us up together, *and made us sit together in heavenly places in Christ Jesus*" (Eph. 2:4-6)? In union with a transcendent Lord, we are enthroned in heavenly places, where our ministry of intercession can be the exercise of a royal priesthood.

Joshua Commissioned

"And the angel of the Lord protested unto Joshua, saying, Thus saith the Lord of hosts; If thou wilt walk in my ways, and if thou wilt keep my charge, then thou shalt also judge my house, and shalt also keep my courts, and I will give thee places to walk among these that stand by. Hear now, O Joshua the high priest, thou, and thy fellows that sit before thee ... behold, I will bring forth my servant the BRANCH." This was God's great commission given to His child. Until the Branch appeared, the faithful had to continue in holy office. This ministry would be a means of grace to Israel, and an example to fellow men. We are reminded of the commission given to us, "Occupy till I come." Zechariah's vision embodies the main features of God's salvation. All ministers should emulate this example. We must stand in the holy place before we stand in the pulpit, for only thus can we efficiently present the amazing wonder of our superlative message.

CHRIST . . . and His gracious invitation
(MATTHEW 11: 28)

As the blackness of the night sky seems to be studded with fiery gems, so the Bible seems set in rubies and beryl and diamonds, which scintillate and relieve the sombre setting of human failure. And as here and there in the constellations some stars outshine others in brilliance, so certain texts appear to possess added lustre and singular beauty. They are rare gems of incalculable worth, and could not be purchased with a king's ransom. Not the least among these great verses is Matthew 11:28, "Come unto me, all ye that labour and are heavy laden, and I will give you rest." There the entire purpose of Christ's coming is expressed in a few lines; how the aches of a sick world may be removed, and the innate needs of all races fully met.

The Simplicity of the Invitation

The Lord Jesus said, "*Come* unto me. . . ." In contrast to many of the tiresome requirements of ancient orders and modern sects, the word of Jesus is both refreshing and illuminating. *Come* is the first word in every man's vocabulary. Expressed by the outstretched arms of a mother, it conveys meaning when sounds are confusing and irritating. Comparative religions declare that man must *do* or *go*; that eternal rest depends upon the efficiency with which he performs the allotted task. Christ said, *Come,* and His invitation was constantly reiterated. To Peter He said, Come ye after me, and I will make you to become a fisher of men." When the disciples were weary with acts of service, He said, "Come ye apart, and rest awhile." None of these invitations ever led to disappointment. The disciples could draw near to their Lord without moving an inch. So can we—if we know how.

The Scope of the Invitation

The Lord Jesus said, "Come unto me, all ye that labour *and are heavy laden,"* and in that one striking utterance His words circumnavigated a globe. Problems are never sent into exile; their roots go deep in the soil of every country. The cares of this world are common both to palace and hovel; to nobleman and peasant; to university professor and untutored heathen; to the African who sits alone in a hut in the forest, and to the skilled engine driver who sends his screaming train toward the distant horizon. Thus did John write, "For God so loved the world. . . ." *All* who labour and are heavy laden—with care, with fear, with toil—may respond to the invitation of Christ, and be certain to receive a welcome.

The Surety of the Invitation

The Lord Jesus said, "Come unto me, all ye that labour and are heavy laden, and I *will* give you rest." Life is filled with disappointments, and even the most reliable projects have a habit of failing. It is a most humiliating thing to place one's confidence in the promises of a person or movement only to discover at a most crucial moment that one's trust has been misplaced. A covenant is an undertaking in which two parties enter into sacred agreement to abide by the terms of the contract. The Lord Jesus said, "Come unto me . . . and I will give you rest." That promise has been subject to the tests of time and circumstance, yet during the long interval which has elapsed since He first uttered the words, no voice has ever charged Him with inability to honour His promise. The promises of God are always true, always reliable, always a very sound investment.

The Sublimity of the Invitation

The Lord Jesus said, "Come unto me . . . and I will give you *rest*." If this text be a rare jewel of the sky, this word is one of its most delightful facets. It reflects glowing fires of beauty. Turn the jewel in the hand, and the word *rest* will send forth beams of sheer loveliness to delight the heart and thrill the soul. Rest cannot be bought with earth's currency, for it is of God. It is not advice freely given; it is not sympathy sincerely expressed; it is not financial assistance benevolently offered. Rest is healing for a wounded heart, comfort for a troubled mind, fellowship for a lonely spirit, unspeakable relief for a haunted soul. Rest is dawn after midnight, calm after storm, laughter after tears, glad reunion after heart-breaking separation. Rest is heaven's gift to a weary world. No government can supply it; no engineer can manufacture it; no church can claim a monopoly on its distribution. It belongs exclusively to Christ, and He alone can give it to others. He said, "Come unto me . . . and I will give you rest." No night sky is completely clouded if one star is visible, and likewise no life is completely dark if the unrivalled brilliance of this celestial jewel can be seen shining from God's book.

THE HOLY SPIRIT . . . and the unpardonable sin

(MATTHEW 12: 22-32)

The Lord Jesus said, "Wherefore I say unto you, All manner of sin and blasphemy shall be forgiven unto men: but the blasphemy against the Holy Ghost shall not be forgiven unto men. And whosoever speaketh a word against the Son of man, it shall be forgiven him: but whosoever speaketh against the Holy Ghost, it shall not be forgiven him, neither in this world, nor in the world to come" (vv. 31, 32). This great utterance often leads to error and fear. In various parts of the world, despairing people have confessed their terror because they believe they have committed the unpardonable sin. The judgment of God appears to be a guillotine. The eternal death sentence has already been passed, and life is but the interim before the execution takes place. These poor people are utterly miserable, very foolish, and do not understand the Scriptures.

An Unaccepted Testimony

All who believe they belong to this category should consider the circumstances in which Christ uttered these words. He had just delivered a man possessed of a devil, and excitement prevailed among the onlookers. "But when the Pharisees heard it, they said, This fellow doth not cast out devils, but by Beelzebub the prince of the devils" (v. 24). They recognized that Christ was the medium through whom power was manifested, but they failed to recognize whence that power came. In actual fact, the last Adam had been manifested to show the fallen first Adam what might be accomplished when man fully surrenders to God the Holy Spirit. Thus it is written that Christ was born of the Spirit—led of the Spirit—returned in the power of the Spirit—spake of the Spirit—and ultimately offered Himself to God through the Spirit. When men ascribed to Satan the deeds of the Holy Spirit, they endangered their souls. The Lord realized that soon a major change would take place in the workings of God. He Himself would return to heaven, in order that the Comforter might come to earth as the representative of the Godhead. He would have a unique commission, and would constantly witness of Christ. "Howbeit when he, the Spirit of truth, is come, he will guide you into all the truth: for he shall not speak of himself . . . He shall glorify me: for he shall receive of mine, and shall show it unto you" (John 16: 13, 14). Christ knew that many people would reject this testimony.

An Unending Tragedy

If the Divine Spirit constantly affirms the truth of redemption as found in Christ; if as Christ taught, "He shall receive of mine, and shall show it unto you "—if this ministry came forth from God the Father, and men rejected it, what more could be done for them? Christ was God's answer to human need. The Holy Spirit was God's method of bringing Christ to human need. To reject His message, to spurn Christ, would mean immeasurable guilt. Since Christ alone can deal with human sin, a man without Christ must remain unpardoned. Thus the statement was made: "It shall not be forgiven him, neither in this world, neither in the world to come." The unpardonable sin is the rejection of the Lord Jesus Christ. Language is inadequate to express the disaster of a lost soul.

An Unnecessary Terror

When God finally abandons man, all spiritual promptings will cease. The soul will be dead; the opportunities gone for ever. When a man is worried about this matter, it is evident that some power is at work in his consciousness. A whisper says, "You need Christ," and fear responds, "It's too late now; you have committed the unpardonable sin." Whence came the first whisper? If God has departed, would He return to torment the guilty soul? If the prompting be heard, there is reason to believe that God is still seeking the man's soul. The objection represents Satan's greatest effort to thwart the purposes of God in the man's salvation. It may be safely assumed that *all who have committed the unpardonable sin are not in the least worried about it.* The souls who are tormented by such thoughts have the least reason to fear. If God has come near enough to whisper "Jesus," He cannot be far away. Let us kneel to pray, and the sunshine will shine through the clouds. God is a Father, a wonderful Father—not a tyrant!

THE GOLD DIGGER ... and the way he staked his claim

(MATTHEW 13: 44)

" Again, the kingdom of heaven is like unto treasure hid in a field ; the which when a man hath found, he hideth, and for joy thereof goeth and selleth all that he hath, and buyeth that field." This text is based upon the fact that in ancient times banks were unknown in the Middle East. During Bible days men had to be their own bankers, and this led to the practice of burying treasure in the ground. No one thought of hiding valuables at home, for in the event of a Philistine raid whole villages could be destroyed by fire. Even to-day men can be seen digging around the remains of ancient buildings in the hope of finding wealth. Such men could be seen any day during the Lord's ministry ; and inspired by such a sight, Christ delivered one of His most picturesque sermons. He said, "The kingdom of heaven is like unto treasure hid in a field."

The Man Seeking

Probably the finder had first heard about buried treasure when he was a little child. His mother told romantic stories which thrilled his heart, but these tales had been allowed to remain dormant in his mind. Now the boy had become a man, and with increasing interest had decided to test the validity of the account so often repeated. Armed with his spade he went forth to dig, and his first discovery revealed far more dirt than treasure. When he commenced his work, critics laughed him to scorn. The Lord Jesus declared that the kingdom of heaven was like that. God's treasures are not always found on the surface. It would appear that an evil hand has covered them. Enemies of the Christian faith glibly declare that seekers after eternal treasure will be more likely to find hypocrites. Their remarks accentuate the fact that to find spiritual wealth, man needs to look beyond dirt.

The Man Sacrificing

Ignoring the jibes of the onlookers, the digger proceeded with his task, and suddenly discovered the buried box. Careful investigation revealed that this was no hallucination. The story heard from childhood was true. Then a new problem appeared. He asked, "How can I make this mine?" Jesus continued, " ... the which when a man hath found, he hideth, and for joy thereof goeth and selleth all that he hath, and buyeth that field." We see the man selling his cottage, his clothing, his possessions; and if at the end of the sale he required extra money, he earned it with the labour of his hands. Carefully preserving the secret of his motives, the man appeared to be the greatest fool in the place. When he gave all his possessions in exchange for a field, his fellow citizens probably pronounced him insane. He merely smiled, for he realized that no sacrifice could be too great under these special circumstances. And the Lord said, "The kingdom of heaven is like that." Let a man discover reality in the Gospel, and the criticisms of a crowd will be meaningless.

The Man Succeeding

The business transaction was completed in the presence of the elders, and the news of the purchaser's lunacy became the talk of the place. Perhaps people followed him, and wondered what he intended to do with his property. Did the man borrow his neighbour's spade, or did he dig with his hands? The earth was thrown from the hiding place, and once again the treasure was uncovered. The astonished crowd gasped, for while they jested he had become rich. Within a little while his cottage was replaced by a mansion; his old garments were superseded by those of a prince. And Jesus said again, "The kingdom of heaven is like that." Let a man ignore the sneers of his fellow men; let a man look beyond what might appear to be hypocritical dirt; let a man seek wholeheartedly for God, and soon he will uncover eternal riches. The gold of grace, the pearls of promise, the rubies of redemption, and wealth from an everlasting realm will reward his efforts. The old cottage of mortality will be replaced by immortality; the corruptible will put on incorruption; and from poverty, the finder will be transported to realms of enchanting wonder. Yes, the kingdom of heaven is like unto treasure hid in a field, the which when a man hath found, he hideth, and for joy thereof goeth and selleth all that he hath, and buyeth that field. Gold diggers and diamond hunters need excellent eye-sight. The entire purpose of their activities may be thwarted if they allow too much dirt to get into their eyes!

THE FUNERAL OF JOHN ... and its glorious sequel
(MATTHEW 14: 12)

Beneath the stout grey walls of a king's palace in Caesarea was a little cell; it was dark and gloomy, and probably damp. Outside the door stood a soldier, placed there to prevent any rescue of the imprisoned John Baptist. And overhead the stars shone down on a festive night, when a king's birthday celebrations were about to ruin his soul. John sat on his prison bench and thought of the morrow. His disciples would bring news of the outside world—a world he had not known for eighteen months. The prisoner's eyes saw in retrospect those soul-thrilling meetings in the Jordan valley, when God's blue sky had been as a roof in his open-air cathedral; when the congregations lined the river bank and heard the words of life. Ah! and John sighed. It seemed tragic that Herod's inexcusable sin had interfered with such a promising revival. Eighteen months of imprisonment had been poor reward for faithful service; yet John Baptist smiled. It was better to be imprisoned for faithfulness than to be free and useless in God's service. Yes, to-morrow his followers would be visiting him.

The Hour of Need Restored Their Humility

They were coming, but their steps seemed to drag—the steps of weary men. Calamity had ruined their happiness. How wonderful had been the past; yet those days would never return. Why had God sent their fearless master to denounce the sin of Herod? Would it not have been better had he continued to preach to thousands of waiting people? If John had acted correctly in denouncing Herod, why had his example not been followed by Jesus of Nazareth? His disciples were having a grand time, while they were left stranded through the imprisonment of their beloved leader. They frowned as they remembered the other men. Their different outlooks had occasioned argument, and strife had been avoided only by the narrowest of margins. Ah well, they would be able to tell John all about it. They reached the door—it was unguarded and open. What did this mean? Hurriedly they entered, to stand horror-stricken at the scene. Their master had been beheaded; the floor was stained with scarlet. " And his disciples came and took up the body, and buried it...." They found a sheltered spot, where they dug a grave. Reverently and with great tenderness they laid the body of John to rest, and even the strongest of them wept at the ceremony. When the task was completed they mutely looked at each other, and their unspoken question was expressed in every eye. What can we do now? And in that cruel hour of sorrow the voice of the Holy Spirit whispered, " Go and tell Jesus."

The Hour of Need Revealed His Grace

They stood around as one of their number told the Saviour about their grim discovery. After all, they had belonged to a rival group; they might have had much in common, but just a trace of jealousy had coloured their own outlook, and some of the Carpenter's disciples had long memories. The Lord gravely listened, and the charm of His gracious personality laid their fears to rest. Yes, He was very glad they had come to tell Him of their sorrow. He was very sympathetic—He was more. They could not express all they felt, but somehow they knew He understood. The shadows disappeared from their eyes; they felt happier, and then they listened, for He was speaking to them. He seemed to appreciate their problems, and in an indefinable way He was easing the ache in their hearts.

The Hour of Need Solved Their Problems

Did the Lord invite them to stay with Him? We are given a detailed description of the call and ordination of the original twelve disciples; but such information is not forthcoming in regard to the additional fifty-eight disciples who increased the number of followers to seventy. Were the disciples of John among the new acquisitions? Since the tragic day when John's followers poured out their petitions and confessed their sorrows before Christ, millions of fellow disciples have done likewise; and in every case, Christ has been sufficient. Burdens become less heavy when they are shared with the Lord Jesus, and even the dread fears of an uncertain future disappear when an anxious disciple learns to rest in a Saviour's love. " Let us therefore come boldly . . . that we may obtain mercy, and find grace to help in time of need." " Jesus Christ the same yesterday, and to-day, and for ever " (Heb. 14:16 ; 13:8).

THE SILENCE OF CHRIST ... which preached to a world
(MATTHEW 15: 21-23)

"Never man spake like this man" was one of the most striking things ever uttered concerning Christ; and the helplessness of the officers who were sent to arrest the Lord Jesus, ably endorsed their verdict. Words of profound wisdom fell from the Teacher's lips, and it was said that He spoke as one having authority and not as the scribes. Eloquence and wisdom, simplicity and profundity, clarity of thought, directness of approach, tenderness and fearlessness all combined to place Him in a class of His own. Yet in strange contrast was the astounding fact that sometimes His silence was more effective than His sermons. Often when circumstances demanded an oration, He calmly considered the matter and then refused to speak.

He was silent when we would expect Him to answer prayer

"And behold, a woman of Canaan came out of the same coasts, and cried unto him, saying, Have mercy on me, O Lord, thou son of David; my daughter is grievously vexed with a devil. But he answered her not a word." This action was apparently inexplicable, but it brought the very best out of the woman's soul. Her faith was tried, and ultimately she went away a better woman. If the Lord immediately and unconditionally answered every prayer, more harm than good would result. Sometimes He accomplishes most by refusing to grant our desires. (See *Bible Cameos*, p. 91.)

He was silent when we would expect Him to defend a woman
(John 8:6)

When the enemies of Christ brought to Him the woman taken in adultery, they said, "Master, this woman was taken in adultery, in the very act. Now Moses in the law commanded us, that such should be stoned: but what sayest thou? This they said, tempting him, that they might have to accuse him. But Jesus stooped down, and with his finger wrote on the ground, as though he heard them not...." And we know now that His silence delivered Him from a foul plot. (See *Bible Cameos*, p. 137.) Words spoken in haste are often repented at leisure, and very frequently it is the still tongue that makes a wise head. The Master's silence enabled Him to consider the grave issues at stake; and when at length He answered His critics, His words exhibited great wisdom. His was the most eloquent silence ever known.

He was silent when we would expect Him to continue preaching (John 4:1-3)

"When therefore the Lord knew how the Pharisees had heard that Jesus made and baptized more disciples than John ... He left Judea, and departed again into Galilee." There is reason to believe that this was one of the most suggestive of all His actions. When the blessing of God was falling in increasing measure, when people were responding to the call of the Gospel, when revival knocked at the door, He quietly withdrew from the scene and allowed John Baptist to continue the great work. He knew that the enemies were beginning to compare the two camps, and soon their evil tongues would be saying that rivalry existed between Christ and His forerunner. Before they had the chance to begin, the Lord graciously went to another district.

He was silent when we would expect Him to defend Himself (Matt. 27:12-14)

"And when he was accused of the chief priests and elders, he answered nothing. Then said Pilate unto him, Hearest thou not how many things they witness against thee? And he answered him to never a word; insomuch that the governor marvelled greatly." (i) Christ was careful not to make others sin. (ii) He was patient in bearing reproach. (iii) He was willing to endure all things—even a cross—if by so doing He could honour God and help His fellow men. What would we have done in similar circumstances? Pilate marvelled—and probably all heaven marvelled with him.

He was silent when facing a guilty soul (Luke 23:8, 9)

"And when Herod saw Jesus, he was exceeding glad: for he was desirous to see him of a long season, because he had heard many things of him; and he hoped to have seen some miracle done by him. Then he questioned him in many words; but he answered him nothing." And thereby hangs a tale—a tale of tragedy and sin. God once declared: " My Spirit shall not always strive with man," and Herod provided the infamous example of this fact. He had murdered John Baptist, and had thereby sealed his destiny. Even the great lover of souls had no word of rebuke, of love, or even of advice. He let him die. " He answered him nothing," and that silence preached a sermon which still echoes around the world.

CHRIST . . . and the eternal bulldozer
(Matthew 17: 19, 20)

"Then came the disciples to Jesus apart, and said, Why could not we cast the devil out? And Jesus said unto them, Because of your unbelief: for verily I say unto you, If ye have faith as a grain of mustard seed, ye shall say unto this mountain, Remove hence to yonder place; and it shall remove; and nothing shall be impossible unto you." Faith is heaven's bulldozer which removes every obstacle and makes a highway to the throne of God. Yet faith is far more than an intellectual assent. It is a vital apprehension of things unseen; it laughs at impossibilities.

No Faith

The ship was sinking, and even the experienced fishermen were scared. Their skilled seamanship was unequal to the task of keeping the small vessel on an even keel, and at any moment the frail craft might capsize in the turbulent waters. The winds shrieked through the rigging; the mast threatened to break. Frantic baling made little impression on the swirling waters in the bottom of the boat; the position was untenable. The fishermen disciples were beginning to despair, when they remembered their Master. They could hardly believe their eyes when they saw Him peacefully sleeping in the back of the boat. "And they awake him, and say unto him, Master, carest thou not that we perish? And he arose, and rebuked the wind, and said unto the sea, Peace, be still. And the wind ceased, and there was a great calm. And he said unto them, Why are ye so fearful? How is it that ye have *no faith*?" (Mark 4: 37-40).

Little Faith

A remarkable stillness rested upon the holy hill; the crowd was enthralled. This was the greatest sermon they had ever heard. Slowly, but with rare power, the Preacher from Nazareth spoke about faith. "Therefore I say unto you, Take no thought for your life, what ye shall eat, or what ye shall drink; nor yet for your body, what ye shall put on. Is not the life more than meat, and the body than raiment?" He paused, and the ensuing silence was as eloquent as His speech. No one moved; no one desired to move. This was wonderful preaching. He was so sure. He really believed what He was saying; and what was much more to the point, He had the ability to make them believe. Their emotions were strangely stirred. He continued, "And why take ye thought for raiment? Consider the lilies of the field, how they grow ; they toil not, neither do they spin : And yet I say unto you, That even Solomon in all his glory was not arrayed like one of these. Wherefore, if God so clothe the grass of the field, which to-day is, and to-morrow is cast into the oven, shall he not much more clothe you, O ye of *little faith*?" (Matt. 6:25-30). It is very foolish to worry when the promises of God are so reliable.

Great Faith

The Lord Jesus was very interested ; something unique had taken place. The elders of the synagogue had swallowed their pride in seeking a favour, but all their plans had been ruined by the very man on whose behalf they had acted. They had persuaded Christ to visit the home of the Gentile officer ; but now, he had said, " Lord, trouble not thyself : for I am not worthy that thou shouldest enter under my roof . . . say in a word, and my servant shall be healed." Master, because I represent Caesar's empire, I command men to do things, and they obey. You represent God's empire, and if you issue a command, that will be sufficient. Some angel will hasten to do your bidding, and my servant shall be healed. " When Jesus heard these things, he marvelled . . . and said . . . I have not found so *great faith,* no, not in Israel " (Luke 7 : 1-10).

In the spiritual realm, the Capernaum centurion had a twin sister—she was the woman of Canaan who tried to deceive the Lord. (See *Bible Cameos,* p. 91.) She clung to the belief that Christ would help her, even though her appeals for help met with no immediate response. " But he answered and said, I am not sent but unto the lost sheep of the house of Israel. Then came she and worshipped him, saying, Lord, help me. But he answered and said, It is not meet to take the children's bread and cast it to dogs. And she said, Truth, Lord : yet the dogs eat of the crumbs which fall from their masters' table. Then Jesus answered and said unto her, O woman, *great is thy faith*: be it unto thee even as thou wilt. And her daughter was made whole from that very hour " (Matt. 15 : 22-28). Faith is a great bulldozer—it can remove mountains. But what is faith? Someone has supplied a most illuminating acrostic: F A I T H—*F*orsaking *A*ll *I T*ake *H*im. These texts placed together represent the royal highway. No motor traffic travels there. Travellers must walk— by faith ; and those who walk by faith, walk with God.

THE GREAT WEDDING . . . and the people who came late

(MATTHEW 25: 1-13)

"And as he sat upon the mount of Olives, the disciples came unto him privately, saying, Tell us, when shall these things be? and what shall be the sign of thy coming, and of the end of the age?" (Matt. 24:3). By parable and preaching the Lord granted their request, and instructed them regarding His return. He warned them not to be deceived by false prophets; He urged them not to be weary in well-doing; and finally, in short thought-provoking illustrations, He described the Church of the future.

The Certainty of His Return

"Watch therefore, for ye know neither the day nor the hour wherein the Son of man cometh." As the Lord drew near to His death and departure from this world, He constantly repeated the promise of His second advent, and His statement harmonized perfectly with other prophetical utterances. At His birth the promise had been given, " He shall be great, and shall be called the Son of the Highest: and the Lord God shall give unto him the throne of his father David: And he shall reign over the house of Jacob for ever; and of his kingdom there shall be no end " (Luke 1:32, 33). It need hardly be said that this promise was never fulfilled during His ministry on earth. The throne of David was in Jerusalem, where Christ received a cross and not a crown. Messianic prophecies referred to an earthly kingdom, and these predictions have never been fulfilled. The angels repeated the promise immediately after Christ's ascension (Acts 1:10, 11), and this teaching became the hope and message of the early Christian Church (1 Thess. 4:16-18; 1 John 3:2).

The Conformity to His Requirements

"Then shall the kingdom of heaven be likened unto ten virgins, which took their lamps, and went forth to meet the bridegroom. And five of them were wise, and five were foolish." It has been said that this is one of the greatest of Christ's parables. Here two classes are seen in bold relief. All ten virgins believed in the coming of the bridegroom, and hoped to be present at the marriage reception. The entire party waited for the glad event; but in the moment of testing, five virgins were found to be unprepared to meet the bridegroom. Their lamps were going out! It is a cause for regret that hours had been wasted in sleeping, when a few minutes' work might have avoided a tragedy. The foolish virgins remind us of a vast host of modern people. Even the wise virgins were content to sit at ease and to slumber when at their very elbows were people in urgent need. It is not sufficient to believe in Christ's return: we must be ready for His appearing. None can deny that a large proportion of Christendom is filled with dead formalism. There are many custodians of the lamp, but not much light!

The Calamity of His Rejection

"And . . . the bridegroom came; and they that were ready went in with him to the marriage: and the door was shut. Afterward came also the other virgins, saying, Lord, Lord, open to us. But he answered and said, Verily I say unto you, I know you not. Watch therefore, for ye know neither the day nor the hour wherein the Son of man cometh." There is nothing to suggest that the door of opportunity was ever re-opened. The people who might have been rejoicing in the presence of the bridegroom were left to mourn in the shadows of the night. Three thoughts demand expression. (i) *A belated request.* "Lord, Lord, open to us." Had there been adequate preparation the need for this prayer would have been unknown. Hours of self-confidence had ruined priceless opportunities. (ii) *A bewildering response.* "I know you not." Self-esteem could not become a key to open the closed door. The Lord had disowned them, and His verdict was final. On another occasion He spoke of some who would say in the day of judgment, "I have preached in thy name," and again His response was, "I know you not." (iii) *A bitter remorse.* ". . . there shall be weeping." Jesus said, "Be ye also ready." Many Bible teachers believe the coming of Christ to be imminent. They may be correct in their deductions, and it behoves every Christian to attend to his lamp and thus be assured of personal readiness to meet the Lord. When the door of heaven closes it stays closed for a long time. It is far easier to walk through an open doorway, than it is to force a lock!

CHRIST ... and the tale of two cities
(MARK 6: 7-12)

The synagogue was in an uproar; the citizens of Nazareth were angry! It was disgraceful that their one-time carpenter should have defiled the holy place with his abominable utterances. He had a swollen head—he was an arrogant young fool—he was a disgrace to his parents and the community in general. He should have been thrown over the precipice, but perhaps it was providential that he had escaped. The good name of Israel might have been stained with murder. Good riddance to him! And outside the city of sin, the Lord Jesus sorrowfully looked back at His old home, and sighed. "And he called unto him the twelve, and began to send them forth by two and two...." They were ready to depart when He reminded them of two cities.

The City of Disgusting Passion

Lot sat in the gateway of the ancient city, and watched the approach of two strangers. Where would they spend the night? They were in danger, but were unaware of the perils of entering Sodom. He would offer them shelter. "Gentlemen, follow me quickly, or else—Ah, we are too late. That devilish mob saw us. Excuse me, I'll be back in a moment." And he closed the door behind him. Poor man, he has gone to turn wolves from their victims. The angels opened the door to pull him to safety. He was rather startled, but outside, the lewd cries of filthy men echoed through the night. Hell was abroad! Those beastly men were a blot on God's fair world. "Then the Lord rained upon Sodom and upon Gomorrah brimstone and fire from the Lord out of heaven." When the disciples shuddered, the Saviour reminded them of the other place—

The City of Dignified Pride

"Can you see it, children? It has elaborate, ornate synagogues, and the elders are men of standing. They fast twice in the week, and give tithes of all they possess. They are dignified, and true to the traditions of the fathers. Yet, watch them now, as two preachers begin to speak in the market place. They frown. 'What is this? Repent! Good gracious! Are those itinerant evangelists telling us to repent? Disgraceful! We are children of Abraham. Hidden sin in our hearts! Such unwarranted interference and cheek. Preacher, mind your own business, and repent of your own wickedness. And leave our city; we don't want your noise nor your religion.'"

Jesus paused to ask, "Can you see those two cities? Now listen again, 'And whosoever shall not receive you, nor hear you, when ye depart thence, shake off the dust under your feet for a testimony against them. Verily I say unto you, *It shall be more tolerable for Sodom and Gomorrah in the day of judgment, than for that city.*'"

(i) *The Day of Judgment—how sure*

Unless there be a day of final reckoning, this statement of Christ is utterly misleading. This part of His teaching coincides with His other messages. He believed that ultimately all men will stand before God, to account for the things done in this world. He believed, too, that men could be lost; and it was to save such people He came into the world.

(ii) *The Decision of the Judge—how surprising*

Why should Sodom have a better chance than the city of a later date? Sodom had no Gospel, no preachers to warn of the consequences of sin, no church where services were held. Sodom had never heard of the Lord Jesus, and had never witnessed His amazing miracles. The other city had heard of Christ, had met His ambassadors, had seen the miracles of redeeming grace—and had no excuse for ignorance. God can only judge a man according to the light which he possesses.

(iii) *The Desires of Jesus—how sincere*

"And they went out, and preached that men should repent. And they cast out many devils, and anointed with oil many that were sick, and healed them." The Lord Jesus desired to save men. He wanted them to hear the way of truth, and be unashamed before the throne of God. Have I heard the Gospel? Have I ever been challenged with the importance of deciding for Christ? Have I been reared in a godly home and a Christian Church? Could it be possible that in the day of judgment it will be more tolerable for untutored, black heathen, than it will be for me?

> When I soar to worlds unknown,
> See Thee on Thy judgment throne;
> Rock of Ages, cleft for me,
> Let me hide myself in Thee.

CHRIST . . . and a unique sense of values
(MARK 8: 36; LUKE 7: 28; EPHESIANS 3: 8)

God's simple equations are astounding; His sense of values is something to cause amazement. He relegates the great things of earth to a place of insignificance, and lifts the unattractive to a place of importance. God's way of working is often bewildering, and this simple study in compounding values illustrates this fact.

The Unequalled Greatness of Man

The world in which we live is a treasure house of beauty. The Supreme Architect gave of His best when He fashioned and executed His plans concerning the universe. This planet is but one of untold millions, yet here we find immeasurable riches. The mineral wealth of the coal-fields, the diamond fields, and the gold reefs, is something beyond computation. Centuries ago man began extracting this treasure, but much more remains than he has ever claimed. The earth with its riches, the harvests with their abundant provision, the vast mountain ranges which have been the guardians of the plains from time immemorial, the stately splendour of the forests, and the amazing achievements of man, beggar description. The earth presents an Aladdin's cave of gigantic proportions. The ransoms of a million kings would be but a fraction of its indescribable riches; and yet according to Christ, all this could not equal the value of a soul. The towering hills, the scintillating gems, the radiance of a sunrise, the charm of the sea at eventide, the freshness of the flowers, the roaring industries, the far-flung empires of man are nothing in comparison with the value of a soul. Christ said, " For what shall it profit a man, if he shall gain the whole world, and lose his soul?" (Mark 8:36).

The Unprecedented Greatness of a Saint

We are justified therefore in assuming that from God's viewpoint, man is the crown of creation. He was made in the likeness of God, and is sufficiently great to retain his place. Something of the greatness of God may still be detected in human ability. The realms of music, art, science, have all produced men of genius, beneath whose spell the world has been enthralled. Yet, if we were to harness all the gifts of these illustrious people, and if we could present them to one superman, even he would not represent superlative wealth. Could he paint lifelike scenes which would astonish angels; could he produce music to rival the harmony of heaven's choirs; could he sing with the voice of a seraph; could he read the secrets of the night sky, and forecast unerringly the events of the future—were he astronomer, musician, scientist, artist, millionaire—were he the greatest man in God's world, he would be less than the least Christian. Christ declared of John Baptist, " Among those that are born of women, there is not a greater prophet than John the Baptist: but he that is least in the kingdom of God is greater than he." A prophet was God's man ; the greatest prophet was God's special man ; and yet the weakest, the most uneducated Christian—the LEAST *in* the kingdom of God supersedes the greatest *outside* the kingdom of God. Therefore if a man is of more value than the world, and a saint is greater than the best man, it follows that the world of nature cannot be compared with the wonder of a redeemed soul. God could make another world, and people it with great men and women ; but to produce another Calvary would baffle even the omniscience of the Almighty.

The Unimaginable Greatness of Christ

If one Christian represents such fabulous wealth, the untold millions of saints who form the Church of Christ would represent a correspondingly increased amount. For example, when John described the choir of the redeemed, he said, " The number of them was ten thousand times ten thousand, and thousands of thousands." The Church of Christ is composed of people drawn from " every kindred, and tongue, and people, and nation." Yet in the sight of God, the reconciling death of Christ equalled the need of this immense throng. " For as by one man's disobedience many were made sinners, so *by the obedience of one shall many be made righteous* " (Rom. 5:19). If that which Christ accomplished satisfactorily cancelled the immense debt of so many, then how great was the value of His sacrifice. Perhaps Paul had this thought in mind when he endeavoured to express the wonder of his Lord. Because most adjectives seemed too commonplace, the apostle spoke of " The unsearchable riches of Christ "—and yet, He died for us!

> I stand all amazed at the love Jesus offers me,
> Confused at the grace that so freely He proffers me ;
> I tremble to know that for me He was crucified—
> That for me, a sinner, He suffered, He bled, He died.
>   Oh, it is wonderful that He should care for me
>   Enough to die for me!
>   Oh, it is wonderful, wonderful to me!

FIVE HEADS ... with but a single thought
(Mark 10: 21; John 9: 25; Luke 10: 42; Psalm 27: 4; Philippians 3: 13)

It is far better to have one aim in life, and to achieve an ambition, than to attempt innumerable things and miss them all! Centrality of purpose is always a commendable feature, and it is truly significant that five of the leading Bible characters excelled in this respect. When these are grouped together, we are provided with a sequence of thought which embraces the entire range of Christian experience.

"One Thing Thou Lackest"

When the Lord Jesus told the rich young ruler to keep the Commandments, the earnest seeker replied, "Master, all these have I observed from my youth. Then Jesus beholding him loved him, and said unto him, One thing thou lackest: go thy way, sell whatsoever thou hast, and give to the poor, and thou shalt have treasure in heaven: and come, take up the cross, and follow me. And he was sad at that saying, and went away grieved; for he had great possessions." This illustrious young man possessed everything except that which mattered most. His home was filled with valuables, while his soul remained poor. Life begins when man responds to the call of Christ to take up the cross and follow in the path of discipleship. No amount of money, no degree of popularity, no worldly honours can ever compensate for the loss of eternal treasure.

"One Thing I Know"

The street was filled with people; the religious leaders were protesting against the enthusiasm aroused by the latest miracle of Jesus. The people were fools swayed by every wind of doctrine! This was a storm in a teacup! "Then again called they the man that was blind, and said unto him, Give God the praise: we know that this man is a sinner. He answered and said, Whether he be a sinner or no, I know not: one thing I know, that, whereas I was blind, now I see." In contrast to the rich young ruler, this man was willing to sacrifice anything in order to follow Christ; and his unashamed testimony surely brought joy to the Saviour's heart. Military leaders say that attack is often the best defence. This is true of spiritual warfare.

"One Thing is Needful"

The charming home in Bethany had suddenly become a place of strain. The atmosphere was tense, and there seemed every likelihood of a first-class quarrel. When twenty people were waiting for their meal, and many tasks demanded attention in the kitchen, "Mary sat at Jesus' feet, and heard his word." Martha's patience suddenly failed, and looking into the Lord's face, she said, "Dost thou not care that my sister hath left me to serve alone? bid her therefore that she help me. And Jesus answered . . . thou art careful and troubled about many things: But one thing is needful: and Mary hath chosen that good part, which shall not be taken away from her." Spiritual appetite is always an indication of a healthy soul. In any case, Mary would have been useless in the kitchen, when her heart was in the parlour!

"One Thing Have I Desired"

David's soul was a ship adrift on turbulent waters. Surging emotions played havoc with his peace of mind, and memories of spiritual lapses haunted him. He had reason to believe that "in his body dwelt no good thing"; he had been born in sin and shapen in iniquity; evil was ever present with him. "His heart and his flesh cried out for the living God." Where could he find eternal security? Where could the yearnings of his soul be fully satisfied? When his eyes instinctively turned toward the sanctuary, he cried, "One thing have I desired of the Lord, that will I seek after; that I may dwell in the house of the Lord all the days of my life, to behold the beauty of the Lord, and to enquire in his temple." David might have been the elder brother of Mary of Bethany. They attended the same school—only he was in a higher standard. Of course, after all, he was a bit older!

"One Thing I Do"

It is fitting that Paul, the indomitable missionary, should provide the final link in this chain of spiritual desire. He had graduated in God's school, and was determined to translate his lessons into ceaseless endeavour. He said, "Brethren . . . this one thing I do, forgetting those things which are behind, and reaching forth unto those things which are before, I press toward the mark for the prize of the high calling of God in Christ Jesus." Paul never permitted interference with the realization of his greatest ambitions, and ultimately he was able to say, "I have finished my course . . . henceforth there is laid up for me a crown." To a traveller, one guiding star is better than a million comets which have no meaning.

SIMON THE LEPER ... who remembered to be grateful

(MARK 14: 3)

At the end of his Gospel John wrote, " And there are also many other things which Jesus did, the which, if they should be written every one, I suppose that even the world itself could not contain the books which should be written." Thus in one glorious burst of exuberant eloquence, the beloved disciple endeavoured to express the unlimited scope of the ministry of his Lord. Christians of all ages have wondered about those unrecorded events, and possibly one of the unwritten stories might concern Simon the leper.

His Grief

Leprosy! Dread word! The foul scourge had ruined the life of another Bethany citizen. Poor Simon had been driven from home and family, and had gone into the wilderness. Somewhere outside his town he erected a little shack, where he mourned his misfortune. He was an outcast! He was unclean! He was dead while he still lived. He was known to all the people of Bethany, and among these were Lazarus and his two sisters. Did this family tell Christ about the unfortunate leper? Did the Master listen and go forth in search of the outcast? On the other hand, was Simon the man of whom the Gospels declare, " And behold, there came a leper and worshipped him, saying, Lord, if thou wilt, thou canst make me clean "? Perhaps our questions will remain unanswered until we reach heaven, and then maybe Simon himself will tell us his story.

His Gratitude

The impossible had happened. The Healer had performed the miracle. Simon was no longer a leper. Yet, to distinguish him from the other Simons of Bethany, the people still called him " Simon the leper." They shared his great joy, and were never tired of hearing his testimony. But all the while deep gratitude filled the heart of this earnest disciple. He could never forget that, apart from the mercy of Christ, he would still have been living in the land of shadows outside the city gate. Yes, he would always remember Jesus of Nazareth. And every time the Master visited that other home up the street, Simon wistfully watched and hoped that some day the Saviour would come to his house. Probably Simon's home was a little shabby, for had he not been an outcast? And at last Simon had the courage to mention the matter to Martha and her sister, and his delight was boundless when they promised to arrange the visit. "Lord," they said later, "You remember Simon, the leper whom you cleansed? Well, he wants us all to go to his house to supper, and we promised to take you. Lord, will that be all right? You don't mind, Master, do you?" And Jesus smiled and answered, "Yes, I remember Simon, and I shall be very pleased to visit his home."

His Gladness

Simon was thrilled. The Master was coming down the street, and everything was in readiness for the party. Martha and her sister had helped, and this would be the greatest night of Simon's life. "Oh," he murmured, "if I can only show Him that I'm grateful! If I can only prove to Him that I love Him dearly; that I would gladly give to Him all that I possess. . . . Come in, Master, welcome to my home. I am so pleased you have come." The Lord was smiling. His eyes were pools of delight. "Well, Simon, this is wonderful. Martha told me that you had invited us to supper, and Simon, how shall I ever be able to thank you?" "Lord, how shall you thank me? Oh, Master, it is I who will never be able to thank you. I was a leper until you came." "Ah, Simon, that was a wonderful day, wasn't it? Now I wonder whose delight was the greater, yours or mine?" The simple table was lavishly spread—Martha had seen to that; but Simon was like a schoolboy at his first party. Heaven itself could not have provided greater joys than he knew that night. And when they gathered later in the sitting-room, to listen again to the words of the Lord Jesus, Simon re-lived the day when his miracle had been performed. He watched as Mary broke her box of very precious ointment; he heard again the words of her Lord. Of course he had no box of costly perfume, he only possessed a heart filled with praise; a soul filled with gratitude; and a simple home filled with a great welcome for the Master. And when Jesus looked across at His delighted host, He smiled again, for He knew that Simon the leper and Mary of Bethany were twin souls. They had good memories. They remembered to be grateful. Have we?

PETER . . . who had the shock of his life
(LUKE 5: 1-11)

Simon Peter's second meeting with Christ was momentous. " And it came to pass, that, as the people pressed upon Christ to hear the word of God, he stood by the lake of Gennesaret, And saw two ships standing by the lake: but the fishermen were gone out of them, and were washing their nets. And he entered into one of the ships, which was Simon's, and prayed him that he would thrust out a little from the land. And he sat down, and taught the people out of the ship " (vv. 1-3). This was to become a day of shocks for Simon Peter.

Peter Listening

Gently, the small ship rose and fell on the bosom of the ocean ; and slowly, with skill born of long practice, the fisherman moved his oars backward and forward. The stillness was broken only by the musical waves on the beach, the creaking of the oars in the rowlocks, and the sweet notes of the Teacher's voice. Sometimes He lifted His hand to add emphasis to a part of His message ; sometimes His voice lowered to a whisper ; but even then, His audience seated on the rising beachhead heard every word. And time stood still! The people could have listened for ever. The oars gently dipped in the water ; the boat rose and fell ; the Teacher contentedly sat in the stern. Charming eloquence ; challenging thought ; compassionate entreaty ; irresistible winsomeness : these were the characteristics of His message, and as Simon listened he almost forgot he was controlling the floating pulpit. His movements were automatic.

Peter Learning

A subdued murmur arose from the congregation. The service had ended. People were beginning to stand, and smiles of appreciation were on many faces. The Preacher was turning around on His seat in the stern—"Thank you very much, Mr. Fisherman." His eyes were alight with pleasure. " Now launch out into the deep, and let down your nets for a draught. I always like to compensate people who help me in my work, and your willingness to lend me this boat meant a great deal to me. Let us move into deeper water, and let down the *nets*." And poor Simon frowned. The Teacher was so appreciative, but—" Master, we have toiled all the night and have taken nothing: nevertheless at thy word I will let down the *net*" (vv. 4, 5). Surely the Lord had difficulty in hiding His smile, for He knew Simon was due for a shock. The ship was heading for deep water. *One net* was made ready and allowed to trail as Andrew rowed the boat around in a wide arc. And Jesus watched the entire operation. How delightful! "And when they had done this, they inclosed a great multitude of fishes: and their *net brake.*" "O Simon Peter, what a shame, your good net is breaking. I told you to put down the *nets.*" Silvery wonders were still coming up from the deep; the bottoms of the boats were covered; the piles of flopping fish were getting larger—"And they came, and filled both the ships, so that they began to sink." "Quick, brother Andrew, I'm getting wet; bale water, throw the fish out, row back to the shore."

Peter Languishing

"When Simon Peter saw it, he fell down at Jesus' knees, saying, Depart from me; for I am a sinful man, O Lord. For he was astonished, and all that were with him, at the draught of the fishes which they had taken" (v. 9). Poor Peter! He had lost his morning; he had lost some of his remarkable catch; he had damaged his net; his self-confidence had been shattered. The sermon had weakened his resistance; the fish had destroyed it. This was indeed the Christ, and as Simon looked into the face of the Master his knees gave way, and he cried, "I am a sinful man, O Lord." And Christ gravely watched him. It had taken a great deal of careful planning, much patience, a sermon, a sinking ship, and a shoal of fish, to bring Peter to his knees. *Some legs are very stiff!*

Peter Leaving

"And Jesus said unto Simon, Fear not; from henceforth thou shalt catch men. And when they had brought their ships to land, they forsook all, and followed him" (vv. 10, 11). Their business went into voluntary liquidation. Did they stay long enough to dispose of their fish? What happened to the boat? What did their families say when they went off on what appeared to be a wild goose chase? Peter and his companions never regretted their decision. At Pentecost their net enclosed a very great multitude of fishes— even three thousand, "and for all there were so many, yet was not the net broken." This was the glorious fulfilment of an old promise. "Fear not; from henceforth thou shalt catch men."

THE MAN ... whose right hand was withered
(LUKE 6: 6)

"And it came to pass also on another sabbath, that he entered into the synagogue and taught: and there was a man whose right hand was withered." This is a typical Doctor Luke text, and the beloved physician carefully points out that it was the man's right hand and not his left which was useless. The fellow was very much alive; and as far as we can judge from the Scriptures, his eyesight was not impaired. All his trouble centred in that right hand, which would not respond to his will. The right hand is the hand of service, and for most people the loss of this valuable member would be inestimable. A man might endeavour to work with his left hand, but he would never accomplish all he wished to do unless he could also use the other member which dangled helplessly at his side. He reminds us of Christians whose service is not up to standard. They have received eternal life and are no longer dead in sin; they see clearly and discern between true and false teaching; yet in actual service, spiritual paralysis has withered the right hand. The Bible has several illustrations of this type, and from the sacred record we may now learn the causes of this infirmity.

Sinfulness—Luke 5:18-20

"And, behold, men brought in a bed a man which was taken with a palsy . . . and when Jesus saw their faith, he said unto him, Man, thy sins are forgiven thee." This statement seemed out of place, for the unfortunate sufferer had not come seeking the forgiveness of sins. Paralysis had deprived him of much of the joy of living. His problem was not spiritual, but something practical and physical. The Lord Jesus realized that the cause of the man's helplessness was his secret sin. It would appear that somewhere in his past life the sinner had allowed evil to predominate, and physical infirmity had resulted. The Great Physician dealt with the secret sins before He finally removed the irksome malady. Here was a man who could not walk, who could not work, because sin had paralysed him. We are reminded of the outstanding facts of Christian experience. "If a man regard sin in his heart, the Lord will not hear him."

Prayerlessness—Matthew 17:19-21

"Then came the disciples to Jesus apart, and said, Why could we not cast him out? And Jesus said unto them, Because of your unbelief: for verily I say unto you . . . this kind goeth not out but by prayer and fasting." The Lord Jesus revealed eternal truth in that one great statement. While His disciples had slept, He had prayed. Their impotence and failure to cast out the demon provided a strange contrast to the amazing power of their Lord. Omnipotence and impotence were never so near as on that day. Prayer is a great mystery, and we shall never understand all its secrets until life's journey has been completed. Yet the facts of history and the teachings of the Bible agree that prayer—real, believing prayer—is the greatest weapon given by God to man. *Prayer changes the man who prays.* It makes him more usable for the purposes of God. Eloquence may be the machinery, but prayer is the power which drives it. A church without a prayer meeting—is not a church!

Nervousness—John 9:20-22

"The parents of the blind man answered them and said, We know that this is our son, and that he was born blind: But by what means he now seeth, we know not; or who hath opened his eyes, we know not: he is of age; ask him: he shall speak for himself. These words spake his parents, because they feared the Jews: for the Jews had agreed already, that if any man did confess that he was Christ, he should be put out of the synagogue." Thus two cowardly people failed their boy and dishonoured their Lord. We shall never know what great things might have been accomplished that day if those parents had courageously given their testimony. Supposing they had said, "Oh, priest, our hearts have been aching for years. Our boy was blind, and we brought him regularly to the synagogue. Yet you could do nothing for us. As long as we live we shall love the Lord, and thank Him for this miracle." Such a testimony, given in the power of the Holy Spirit, might have performed an even greater miracle than the one already accomplished. Alas, they were too nervous to do their duty. Their right hands were useless, and thus they lost their greatest opportunity.

CHRIST . . . and the requirements of the new life
(LUKE 7: 15; 8: 55; JOHN 11: 44)

The apostle Paul said, "If ye then be risen with Christ, seek those things which are above, where Christ sitteth on the right hand of God. Set your affections on things above, not on things on the earth" (Col. 3:1, 2). This was the best advice ever given to converts, for it was to be expected that when they renounced the old life, the characteristics of the new would be seen daily in their actions. The requirements of the new life are clearly illustrated in the miracles of the Saviour. The Gospel record contains three accounts of His raising the dead; and when these Scriptures are compared, an interesting sequence of thought is discovered.

Confession—Converts should learn to talk for Christ

The city street was strangely hushed; it was a place of mourning. The people watched the sad procession making its way toward the cemetery; and all grieved, for they knew this was the second time death had devastated the same home. First, the husband had been taken; and now the sorrowing widow had lost her only son. She was haggard; she moved as one in a daze, as she followed the bier. The bystanders waited until the funeral had passed, then they too continued their journey. "Now when Jesus was come nigh to the gate of the city, behold, there was a dead man carried out, the only son of his mother, and she was a widow: and much people of the city was with her. And when the Lord saw her, he had compassion on her." Slowly He moved across to her side, and gently resting His hand upon her shoulder, He whispered, "Mother, don't cry." "And he came and touched the bier: and they that bare the young man stood still. And he said, Young man, I say unto thee, Arise. And he that was dead, sat up, *and began to speak*." Resurrection joys would have been marred if the young man had remained dumb for ever. He had a story to tell; and furthermore, it was his duty to tell it.

Communion—Converts should feed on the Bread of Life

The scene in the bedroom was heart-breaking; the little girl was dead. The mother's anguish was pitiable; sobs shook her body. Those who stood near furtively dabbed their eyes; this was a tragedy; the girl was only twelve years of age. And then the door opened to admit Jairus, the girl's father. He had brought Jesus and three disciples. Momentarily the ruler of the synagogue was overcome; his daughter had been the joy of his life. The three disciples silently watched as their Master went across to the bedside, to say, "Little girl, Wake up." They were thrilled when the colour commenced to come back into the ashen cheeks. They saw the eyelids flicker, and then quite suddenly the child was smiling. "And her spirit came again, and she arose straightway: and he commanded *to give her meat."* "Mother," He said, "Give her something to eat. She is hungry, and needs food." In like manner, all who have risen with Christ need spiritual nourishment in order that their health may be maintained. (i) They must feed on the word of God. (ii) They must enjoy fellowship with the people of God. (iii) They must know intimate communion with the Son of God.

Consecration—Converts should walk in newness of life

Lazarus had been in his grave four days, and the hearts of his sisters were very sore as they stood before the sepulchre. They had brought Jesus to see the grave. Suddenly the Lord raised His voice and said, "Lazarus, come forth. And he that was dead came forth, bound hand and foot with graveclothes: and his face was bound about with a napkin. Jesus saith unto them, *Loose him, and let him go."* Had Lazarus remained in his graveclothes, the liberty of the new life would have been seriously curtailed. How could he walk when his feet were tied? How could he work when his hands were bound? How could he speak distinctly when a cloth held his jaws in a vice? The Lord said, "Loose him, and let him go." It was a similar thought which prompted Paul to send his message to the Colossians. Worldliness hinders the freedom of the Spirit. It is the duty of the saint to "lay aside every weight, and the sin which doth so easily beset us, and to run with patience the race that is set before us" (Heb. 12:1). In this way the Christian consummates his confession and communion. When he shakes off the garments of the old life, he is capable of surrendering his feet, hands, and lips, to do the will of God. "If ye then be risen with Christ, seek those things which are above, where Christ sitteth on the right hand of God." There should never be any three-legged race in the Christian experience!

CHRIST . . . and His commentary on preaching
(LUKE 8: 4-15)

The parable of the sower was perhaps the best known of the Saviour's sermons. The Lord explained how the sowing of the seed represented the preaching of the Gospel, and His remarks were both stimulating and challenging.

The Stolen Seed

" A sower went out to sow his seed . . . and it was trodden down, and the fowls of the air devoured it." It was good seed, which was never allowed to germinate and take root. When Christ interpreted this section of His parable, He indicated that in like manner Satan takes the word of Truth from the hearts of people, lest they should believe and be saved. And in that one great statement Christ revealed the setting of Biblical doctrines. Man is at the heart of all spiritual struggle. The object of God's love, and the desire of the great Sower, humanity needs the Word of God ; yet every attempt to sow the good seed in human hearts is challenged by evil. The Pharisees in every Gospel service supply evidence in support of Christ's statement.

The Starved Seed

" And some fell upon a rock ; and as soon as it was sprung up, it withered away, because it lacked moisture." The profession of abundant life was not equalled by its depth of root. The results were superficial ; they were on the surface, and consequently the plant was unable to survive. " These," said Christ, " have no root, which for a while believe, and in time of temptation fall away." Even the Lord had such people among His many followers. At a certain point in His ministry, " they turned back and followed him no more." Real evangelism is recognized by the depth of the work done, and not by its seeming popularity. Judas illustrates this type of follower. He received the word with joy, and appeared to be a most sincere disciple ; yet in the hour of testing he revealed that his profession of faith did not rest on spiritual realities.

The Strangled Seed

" And some fell among thorns ; and the thorns sprang up with it, and choked it." Jesus continued, " These are they which, when they have heard, go forth, and are choked with cares and riches and pleasures of this life, and bring no fruit to perfection." It is not said that the seed failed to germinate; neither is it suggested that a harvest was non-existent. The growth of the plant was seriously hindered, because parasites drained the earth of energy. Every church has its quota of people who belong to this disappointing category. The rich young ruler never brought spiritual fruit to perfection, because his love of riches ruined his spiritual perception. Demas, one of the most promising of Paul's associates, ultimately left the apostle, because the pleasures of the world had attracted his soul. This young man might have become eternally famous; but alas, he disappeared in a wilderness of overgrowing worldliness.

The Successful Seed

"And other fell on good ground, and sprang up, and bare fruit an hundredfold." The disciples easily understood that this kind of seed represented " they, which in an honest and good heart, having heard the word, keep it, and bring forth fruit with patience." And in this way Christ summed up the results of preaching the Gospel. Perhaps every minister should be careful in counting heads; it would be safer to count hearts. Spontaneous responses can be most thrilling, but sometimes the better converts are they who seem reluctant to respond. An uplifted hand is insufficient unless it be propelled by a broken heart. In like manner, every minister should be hesitant before he becomes disheartened. No one sees seed taking root; one must have patience, and learn to believe that the unseen is really taking place. A faithful sower is always of more value than a successful reaper. And if Demas supplied the Biblical illustration for the one type of seed, Timothy may provide the example of the seed well sown. He had "known the holy scriptures from his youth up," and because divine truth had taken root in his heart, the boy grew to be a man of God whose consecrated service influenced a world. The realization that some would be lost did not prevent the farmer from sowing seed. He made allowances for loss by sowing additional seed. We must emulate his example. Let us sow to our maximum capacity; then we shall not enter God's presence empty-handed. The fields are very big; the seed is very plentiful; but there is a shortage of sowers! I wonder why?

THE LAWYER AND THE RULER ... who asked the same question

(LUKE 10: 25; 18: 18)

"What must I do to inherit eternal life?" It is not possible to understand the implications of this text until we appreciate the effect of the preaching of Jesus. Against the uncertainty of the theological thought of His day, His utterances were as stars in a dark sky. The Sadducees and the Pharisees were opposed on the question of survival. The former said that death terminated existence; the latter declared that death was an introduction to another world. And while these leaders argued, the ordinary wayfarer hardly knew what to believe. He saw loved ones taken from his side, but when he considered the possibility of reunion in another world, he could only hope for the best. Then Jesus came to preach in the villages of Galilee, and immediately His bold declarations stirred the hearts of Israel. The Sadducees detested the new doctrines, but the Pharisees were delighted; and it would appear that from these religious camps, two representatives came to ask an identical question. The fact that they received different answers provides food for thought.

The Wise Lawyer

The Sadducees were annoyed. Their teachings were being discounted; their enemies were jubilant. Something had to be done. A clever speaker must challenge the new Teacher. "And behold, a certain lawyer stood up, and tempted him, saying, Master, what shall I do to inherit eternal life? Jesus said unto him, What is written in the law? how readest thou? And he answering said, Thou shalt love the Lord thy God with all thy heart ... and thy neighbour as thyself. And Jesus said unto him, Thou hast answered right: this do, and thou shalt live. But he, willing to justify himself, said unto Jesus, And who is my neighbour?" (Luke 10:25-29). Then the Lord Jesus told the story of the good Samaritan, and finally reminded the man of his duty to go and do likewise. At first, many evangelical teachers would denounce this teaching. Does a man obtain eternal life by fulfilling the requirements of the law? Does a man attain to the highest pinnacle of spiritual possession through self-achievement, when his best righteousness is said to be filthy rags?

The Wealthy Leader

"And a certain ruler asked him, saying, Good Master, what shall I do to inherit eternal life? And Jesus said ...

Thou knowest the commandments . . . And the ruler said, All these have I kept from my youth up" (Luke 18:18-21). It is at this point that the one man differs from the other. How easy it would be to imagine the Lord Jesus saying, "Well done, young man; you have excelled at your learning. Many people really believe that human merit will gain the highest awards in heaven. They say their virtue equals and even excels that of many other people. They keep the law, and challenge any teaching which denies their right to eternal security. Yet you realize this is not true. You are good, but not good enough. You are conscious of spiritual need." And as Christ looked at the departing lawyer, He could have said, "Now that man asked the same question, but his motives were different. If one suggested that he had personal need, he would treat the statement as an insult. He's a lawyer, an expert at discovering flaws in other people. He has yet to discover his own need. You, rich young ruler, know your need. Well done."

The Wonderful Lord

The Saviour continued, "Yet lackest thou one thing: sell all that thou hast, and distribute unto the poor, and thou shalt have treasure in heaven: and come, follow me" (v. 22). Why did not Christ repeat the story of the good Samaritan to this ruler? And why did He not ask the lawyer to forsake all and follow Him? A little investigation reveals the fact that the answers to these questions supply a comprehensive view of the doctrines of God. The lawyer was told to keep the law, for if he conscientiously did this, his very nearness to God would beget a sense of personal need. The ruler had already discovered his need, and it only remained to find a remedy. He was given a new challenge, "Sell all that thou hast, and come, follow me." This was a test to ascertain whether or not he would permit the Lord to occupy the throne of his affections. Probably had he expressed willingness to obey the Master's command, he would have been sent home with a benediction. What must I do to inherit eternal life? I must recognize my need as a sinner, and then crown Christ Lord of my life.

THE HOUSE OF MERCY . . . on the Jericho road

(LUKE 10: 34, 35)

Dear Mr. Inn-keeper,

It seems an awful shame that you should be so hidden amid your surroundings. You are one of the most attractive personalities in the Gospel story. Perhaps it seems a little unfortunate that you should be so closely associated with such a thrilling account, for it is your proximity to Another which rather places you in the shadow. And yet, if you were anywhere else, you would be seen at a disadvantage. Did you build or buy that house on the Jericho road? Surely bravery and wisdom were united in your soul; your nearness to danger provided the opportunity for fame. We have looked at the desolate surroundings of that notorious highway between Jerusalem and Jericho, and have visualized the dramatic scenes of the ambush arranged for the unwary traveller. And then quite suddenly we saw you standing in the doorway of your famous home. You seemed a very nice fellow. What was the name of your hotel? Our eyesight is not too good at this distance, but it looks strangely like " The Sanctuary." Yes, that is a very nice name, and fits admirably into the general pattern of things.

A Wonderful Purpose

Did you help the good Samaritan to carry in the unfortunate victim? We have often read how that wonderful friend " went to him, and bound up his wounds, pouring in oil and wine, and set him on his own beast, and brought him to an inn, and took care of him." Perhaps you had often witnessed such rescues, and had become accustomed to these acts of grace. It would never surprise us if we heard that the good Samaritan was often found on that dangerous highway. Isn't it stupid how self-confident men ignore obvious warnings and calmly walk into trouble? Perhaps you recognized this, and planned a hostel of help. It has just occurred to us to ask— Were you by any chance personally acquainted with the wonderful Samaritan? Were you his friend? He seemed perfectly assured that you would care for his patient and continue his work of healing.

A Wonderful Privilege

Isn't it strange how we sometimes overlook obvious facts? The good Samaritan would have been in difficulty had there been no inn to which he could take his convert—dear me, I'm sorry, Mr. Inn-keeper; that's the trouble with evangelists, we always get your stories mixed up with our message. Now what was I saying? Yes, I remember, your hospitable inn was "The Sanctuary" to which the poor patient was brought. There he was fed and nursed back to life. There during his convalescent days he found a new fellowship; there he saw love in action. Your home was like a glorious church built alongside the highway of life. It seemed providential that it should have been placed in that exact position. The good Samaritan knew its location, and in the hour of need left his precious charge in your care. You helped him. My word, what a great privilege came to you that day!

A Wonderful Promise

Did you accompany this great man to the door on the morning of his departure? Were you sorry to see his going? Ah, but you were sure that he would return, for he said so, didn't he? What does the record say? "And on the morrow when he departed, he took out two pence, and gave them to the host, and said unto him, Take care of him; and whatsoever thou spendest more, when I come again, I will repay thee." Our hearts would have thrilled had we been present that morning. Then, Mr. Inn-keeper, you went indoors and looked after the patient as if he had been your own brother—well, he was, really, wasn't he? You were pleased to notice his returning health. You shook his hand and rejoiced that you had been of service to him and to his great friend. Oh, sir, what happened when the good Samaritan returned? Surely his eyes lit with pleasure when you told him about his convert—oh dear, there I go again. Never mind, you understand what I mean, don't you? Was he pleased? Did he say, "Well done, thou good and faithful servant: inasmuch as ye have done it to him, ye have done it to me"? Were you thrilled with your reward, Mr. Inn-keeper? Now shall I tell you a secret? We are emulating your example, for all Christians have been placed in charge of a similar place of healing. Our Master called it "The Church." It belongs to Him really, but we are privileged to nurse His patients. We are trying to do well, for when He returns we want to be unashamed before Him at His appearing. That's all. Goodbye, Mr. Inn-keeper, and thank you very much.

CHRIST ... who prayed for Peter
(LUKE 22: 31-34)

The atmosphere in the upper room was tense. Incredulity had given place to indignation, and Peter's eyes were expressing the rising feelings of his heart. The other disciples were listening, and Peter resented this statement of his Lord. It was preposterous that He should suggest such a thing. Had he no confidence in His followers? Peter's eyes swept around the little gathering. Almost imperceptibly his chin was pushed out, and his hands became fists. "Lord, what are you saying?" "And the Lord said, Simon, Simon, behold, Satan hath desired to have you, that he may sift you as wheat: But I have prayed for thee, that thy faith fail not: and when thou art converted, strengthen thy brethren." Peter's eyes became pinpoints of anger; his lips pursed, then, "Lord, I am ready to go with thee, both into prison, and to death." His statement was an outburst and a challenge. The other disciples might be unreliable, but he would never disown his Lord. And Jesus quietly answered, "Peter, the cock shall not crow this day, before that thou shalt thrice deny that thou knowest me" ... *But I have prayed for thee.*

The Vision of His Prayer

The Lord Jesus was never taken by surprise, and consequently was never rash in words nor actions. Every major decision in His ministry was preceded by a period of communion, when God gave the guidance so necessary to Christ's inspired ministry. Probably, during one of these times of prayer, the conviction deepened that all was not well with Simon. It became so clear to Him. Peter would slip into the shadows; his hold upon eternal realities would weaken; his future would be in jeopardy! Then the Lord's face revealed the holy determination in His heart. His lips moved and He prayed, and that unrecorded prayer proved to be Peter's lifeline when the coming storm swirled around his soul.

The Virtue of His Prayer

It is noteworthy that the Lord never mentioned the matter to His self-confident disciple until the secret battle had been fought and won. Perhaps other people acquainted with identical knowledge would have uttered loud and persistent condemnations of the unreliable Simon. Within seconds a fiery argument could have filled the little sanctuary with strife. So often, one hasty word has been a match to start a devastating fire, and before the conflagration had been extinguished, blackened scars have appeared on the souls of men and women. This never happened with the Lord Jesus, for His times of prayer were constant safeguards against the activities of evil.

The Value of His Prayer

"When thou art converted, strengthen thy brethren." The Lord Jesus not only saw the approaching tragedy, He looked beyond, to see the new Peter resplendent in the power of a new life. Christ was perfectly certain that His prayer would be answered. He had wrestled in the secret place, and the issue was no longer in doubt. Probably He had no wish to prevent the arrival of the testing time. Rather, he preferred that Peter should undergo the trial, for the disciple would emerge a better and a stronger man. Thus the Lord prayed. We are persuaded that since the ultimate triumph was won in prayer, it was not possible for Simon Peter to be lost. Each time waves of remorse and guilt threatened to sweep the despairing man to oblivion, the strong arms of redeeming love brought him closer to safety.

The Victory of His Prayer

It was all over! A sickening silence had fallen upon the people around the fire; their questionings had ceased. Yet within the mind of a haunted man, a deafening clamour had broken loose. The searing sword of conscience was playing havoc with his peace of mind. Sweeping aside the onlookers, Peter plunged into the night—he had failed, he had disowned his Lord, he was a disgrace! And within the court-house, the Lord was calm. There was no need to worry, for already poor tormented Peter was safe in the arms of a Father's kindness. Later, when the Lord looked down from heaven to see a new man telling forth the word of life on the day of Pentecost, surely His great heart throbbed with thanksgiving; He was so glad He had prayed for Peter. The denial had become a stepping stone to unprecedented triumphs. And because the Lord loves to do things of this nature, He prays for all His followers. There are times when He says, "Father, remember Ivor Powell. Things are becoming difficult and dangerous in his experience." Reader, there are times when He prayers for *you*. I'm thrilled—are you?

CHRIST . . . and the breaking of the bread
(LUKE 24: 35)

Many delightful touches in the ministry of Christ were best seen in retrospect. When the Saviour did certain things, His disciples were often too preoccupied to realize the true value of His actions. Yet in after days, when they reviewed the life of their Lord, they were able to compare spiritual things with spiritual, and see things in their true perspective. They remembered certain little characteristics and said, " Only Jesus could have done that—just like that." And perhaps one of the foremost of these was the way in which He took bread and brake it. It is not without significance that the Emmaus travellers who had failed to recognize the Stranger Christ, confessed afterward " that he was known of them in the breaking of the bread."

A Gracious Parable

" And when he had taken the five loaves and two fishes, he looked up to heaven, and blessed, and brake the loaves, and gave them to his disciples to set before them; and the two fishes divided he among them all " (Mark 6:41). Many years later the disciples remembered the exquisite grace with which He handled the meagre supplies. All through the heat of the day the great crowd had followed Him. Morning had given place to afternoon, and the setting sun had turned the west to crimson. Shadows were lengthening across the fields when Jesus indicated that He desired to feed the hungry. (i) *A Great Scarcity*. It seemed ludicrous to place a little boy's lunch before such a crowd, and the disciples may be excused for muttering, " What are five loaves and two fishes among so many?" (ii) *A Great Saviour*. " He took the loaves, and blessed, and brake them," and immediately thousands of people partook of it and were fed. (iii) *A Great Satisfaction*. When the meal was finished, no one remained hungry unless he had refused to stretch out his hand. Thus did Christ begin to reveal His eternal purpose to feed hungry souls with the bread of life.

A Grim Prediction

" And he took bread, and gave thanks, and brake it, and gave unto them, saying, This is my body which is given for you: this do in remembrance of me " (Luke 22:19). The setting sun had lain down to sleep in its bed of shadows, and the glory that had been day had given way to night. The crowds had gone home and, alone with His disciples, the Lord proceeded to endorse His earlier teaching. He lifted the loaf, and as He divided it He said, "This is my body which is broken for you." With His benediction, He handed the bread to them, and commanded them to eat. They remembered how He had said, "The bread of God is he which cometh down from heaven, and giveth life unto the world. . . . I am the bread of life: he that cometh to me shall never hunger; and he that believeth on me shall never thirst. . . . I am the living bread which came down from heaven: if any man eat of this bread he shall live for ever" (John 6:33-51). And very thoughtfully they lifted the broken bread to their lips.

A Glorious Presentation

"And it came to pass, as he sat at meat with them, he took bread, and blessed it, and brake, and gave to them. And their eyes were opened, and they knew him" (Luke 24:30, 31). Perhaps the vanishing Christ smiled as He left them spellbound at the table. He had put the finishing touches on their tuition; they had graduated at God's university. Did He possess some delightful way in which He handled the bread, or were the nail-prints visible to the watching host and hostess? Excitedly they returned to their colleagues in Jerusalem; but whereas they might have cried, "We saw the wound-prints in His hands," they preferred to say, "He was known to us in the breaking of the bread." In retrospect they saw how that He had thrice acted similarly. Viewed together in their proper sequence, the occasions suggested progression. A gracious parable; a grim prediction; a glorious presentation. He had longed to feed the hungry souls of men and women; He had died to make this possible; He had risen again to finish His task. They realized also that in each of these three scenes, one underlying truth had been important. At the great feast, the hungry people had been required to take the bread from the hand of the disciple-server. At the last supper, they had been required to accept the bread from the hand of their Lord; and outside their little village, the Saviour had continued on His way until they invited Him to enter their home. God may provide a sumptuous banquet, but if my arms be paralysed, I may easily starve.

CHRIST . . . and three steps to a golden throne
(JOHN 1: 39)

"Moreover king Solomon made a great throne of ivory, and overlaid it with the best gold. The throne had six steps, and the top of the throne was round behind: and there were stays on either side of the place of the seat, and two lions stood beside the stays "(1 Kings 10:18, 19). The details of this illustrious piece of furniture suggest that it was one of the most ornate of all Solomon's possessions. The steps which led to the throne remind us of a greater ascent by which we may approach the throne of God. "Behold, a greater than Solomon is here."

Come and See . . . Conversion

The Jordan meetings of John Baptist had taken a new turn. Excitement still prevailed, but the coming of the Carpenter from Nazareth had brought added thrills to the hearts of John's disciples. Of course they adored their leader, but even the Baptist himself spoke reverently of the Newcomer. The thrilling cry, "Behold the Lamb of God, which taketh away the sin of the world" had reverberated across the valley, and still lingered in their hearts. Who was this Jesus? What were His ambitions? Could He be the Messiah? "Again the next day after John stood, and two of his disciples; And looking upon Jesus as he walked, he saith, Behold the Lamb of God! And the two disciples heard him speak, and they followed Jesus. Then Jesus turned, and saw them following, and saith unto them, What seek ye? They said unto him, Rabbi, where dwellest thou? He saith unto them, Come and see. They came and saw where he dwelt, and abode with him that day." How we wish we were able to ask them a few questions! How did the Lord entertain them? What did He say and do during that day? Did they discuss the possibilities of a kingdom? Did He speak to them of God, and the hope of Israel? They were charmed by His kindly hospitality; they heard Him ask blessing upon the meal; His voice was sweetest music. Poor John Baptist! He had lost two of his faithful followers —they had found a new leader. John smiled. It was as he desired. His most fervent wish was to be able to introduce people to Christ.

Go and See . . . Consecration

The day was far spent, and shadows were gathering everywhere. The stars played hide and seek in the sky as the quiet hush of evening descended upon the countryside. Reluctant to leave the great Teacher, the crowd still lingered in His presence. Then the disciples said, "This is a desert place, and now the time is far passed: Send them away, that they may go into the country round about, and into the villages, and buy themselves bread: for they have nothing to eat. He answered and said, Give ye them to eat. . . . How many loaves have ye? *Go and see.* And when they knew, they say, Five, and two fishes" (Mark 6:35-38). The Master blessed the meagre supplies given freely by a small boy, and the wonder of His deed has thrilled a world. Little is much when God is in it, and impossibilities cease to exist when Christ reaches forth His hands. Thousands of people should have been grateful to the child, for his act of consecration supplied all their requirements. The lad became the world's tutor; his example became a standard by which all may judge themselves. What can I bring to Christ? What measure of sacrifice may be found in my giving? My money in Christ's hand might evangelize a million; my talents in Christ's hand might thrill a multitude; my unreservered and unhindered willingness to assist in the work of reaching a hungry world, might delight the heart of God.

O Taste and See . . . Communion

David sat in the mouth of the cave, and recalled his amazing escape from assassination. Truly the Lord had been gracious to him, and all nature harmonized with the deep appreciation of his soul. The rustle of the leaves in the trees was a prelude to a symphony of praise; the wild flowers smiled from their green carpet, and all nature rejoiced. How easy it was to pray; to thank God for unfailing kindness. " O taste and see," cried the psalmist, " that the Lord is good: blessed is the man that trusteth in him " (Psa. 34:8). David had climbed the steps to the throne of God, where he listened to the songs of the eternal. He listened to the strains of infinite loveliness; but when he repeated them, men called him " the sweet singer of Israel." Thus did a king commune with God. Happy is that man who visits Christ and learns to love Him; happier still is that man who desires to help Him in the great work of satisfying the hungry; but happiest of all is that soul who climbs the steps to the throne of God, to sit and commune with his Maker.

ANDREW ... the patron saint of all personal workers

(JOHN 1: 40-42)

Andrew was a go-getter; and if some readers are unfamiliar with this questionable terminology, an explanation will be welcome. A go-getter is a man who stops at nothing. In order to attain his ends he will remove mountains, cross oceans, turn the world inside out, laugh at impossibilities, and finally set a city on fire while other people are looking for a match. A go-getter is a person who goes and gets what he desires, and woe betide anybody who stands in the way. Failure is never admitted, for the untiring man continues until his purpose is fully achieved. Andrew was a man of this calibre. He knew what he wanted, and always took the short cut to reach it. Other men became the great generals in the holy war; but Andrew planned the campaigns, removed the difficulties, and prepared the way for every fresh advance. He was a great go-getter; the patron saint of all who seek souls for Christ.

Andrew First Found Peter

Jesus of Nazareth had been entertaining guests, and one of the privileged visitors was Andrew. He had been standing with John Baptist when the Stranger passed, and hearing John say, " Behold the Lamb of God," Andrew and another disciple had followed Christ. When they received the invitation to accompany the Saviour, they accepted gladly the hospitality of the new Friend, and stayed with Him the whole day. " And one of them which heard John speak . . . was Andrew, Simon Peter's brother. He first findeth his own brother Simon, and saith unto him, We have found the Messiah. . . . And he brought him to Jesus." There was no fuss about this quiet man. He had been with Jesus, and was fully assured that his findings were correct. " *We have found the Messiah* " echoed the certainty of his soul; and that was that! Until this time Andrew took pride of place from his brother Simon. It is interesting to notice that the sacred record says of Bethsaida, " It was the city of Andrew and Peter " (John 1:44). Perhaps he was the elder brother.

Andrew First Found the Lad with the Loaves

When the Lord had gathered together His band of disciples, He separated them into couples in order that their ministry might become more effective. And in the new arrangement, it would appear that Andrew's partner was Philip, for their names are not only coupled together in the official list (Mark 3:18), but these men are seen together also on later occasions. "When Jesus saw a great company come unto him, he saith unto Philip, Whence shall we buy bread, that these may eat?... Philip answered him, Two hundred pennyworth of bread is not sufficient for them, that every one of them may take a little. One of his disciples, Andrew, Simon Peter's brother, saith unto him, There is a lad here, which hath five barley loaves, and two small fishes: but what are they among so many?" (John 6:5-9). Were his eyes alight with expectation as he uttered those words? The provisions were so inadequate that to mention them on such an occasion was an act of stupidity—unless Andrew had very strong reasons for so doing. While the other disciples were regretting their inability to feed the crowd, Andrew was investigating the position. He discovered a boy's lunch. The big man and the small boy pooled their resources, and through them the Master fed a multitude.

Andrew First Brought the Gentiles to Jesus

"And there were certain Greeks among them that came up to worship at the feast: The same came therefore to Philip, which was of Bethsaida of Galilee, and desired him, saying, Sir, we would see Jesus. Philip cometh and telleth Andrew: and again Andrew and Philip tell Jesus" (John 12:20-22). Philip was puzzled. Let us not blame him, for this marked a new departure in the affairs of discipleship. These Greeks were proselytes, but they were still Gentiles. Had they any part in Messianic privileges? Would their inclusion result in troublesome repercussions? "Andrew, what do you think about it?" And when Andrew had shrewdly considered the matter, he replied, "Philip, we'll tell the Master: He'll know what to do." "And Andrew and Philip tell Jesus." And Jesus answered, "The hour is come, that the Son of man should be glorified.... And I, if I be lifted up from the earth, will draw all men unto me." Andrew reminded the Lord of the great world of seeking Gentiles; the Lord gave to Andrew the great privilege of bringing those Gentiles to Him. And perhaps that is the reason why he is now the patron saint of all personal workers for Christ.

THE UNIQUE CHRIST ... and His glorious incomparability
(JOHN 7: 46; LUKE 19: 30; JOHN 19: 41)

"For unto us a child is born, unto us a son is given: and the government shall be upon his shoulder: and his name shall be called, Wonderful, Counsellor, The mighty God, The everlasting Father, The Prince of Peace" (Isa. 9:6). This illuminating prophecy provides the finest Old Testament introduction to the Lord Jesus. No other person could have names such as these, and no other could belong to the same category as He. The Saviour stands alone in splendid magnificence; alone, because by virtue of His person and power He is unequalled.

Unique in His Preaching. "Never man spake like this man"

The leaders of the Jewish nation were very annoyed. They had had enough of this meddlesome Carpenter. They considered His teachings to be obnoxious; His fearlessness was unpardonable arrogance, and the time had arrived to silence the upstart. "... and the Pharisees and the chief priests sent officers to take him" (John 7:32). Poor fellows! They only made one mistake, and we cannot blame them. The people were saying, "When Christ cometh, will he do more miracles than these which this man hath done?" The officers of the law may be excused for the interest which made them linger on the outskirts of the crowd. Probably they planned to arrest Him when the service terminated, when the people had dispersed, and when there was less likelihood of a disturbance among the disciples. As they listened to His message, their hearts were charmed by the power of the preacher. They heard the Lord say, "If any man thirst, let him come unto me, and drink," and as they saw needy people responding to the invitation, they knew this was no ordinary speaker. He was forceful, sincere, fearless. No man spake of God, of eternity, of pardon, as He did. The meeting ended; the officers looked at each other and, helplessly shaking their heads, returned to their masters. When they were asked to explain their conduct they replied, "Never man spake like this man" (v. 46).

Unique in His Power. "... a colt ... whereon yet never man sat"

"And it came to pass, when he was come nigh to Bethphage and Bethany, at the mount called the mount of Olives, he sent two of his disciples, saying, Go ye into the village over against you; in the which at your entering ye shall find a colt tied, *whereon yet never man sat*: loose him and bring him hither" (John 19:29, 30). And all who are acquainted with the fury of unbroken animals regard this feat with amazement. It is not easy to break the resistance of a young colt. Until man has mastered it, its resentment can be volcanic. Yet in the presence of Christ, this unbroken colt was perfectly docile. And when the Lord calmly sat on its back, the little beast probably lifted a proud head and rejoiced in the privilege of carrying the Lord of Creation. No other man could have acted similarly. Many accomplished riders would have succeeded in staying in the saddle, but no other man could have instantly subdued the natural rebellion of the young animal. Could it be that the last Adam was demonstrating the power which God had given to the first Adam? (Gen. 1:26). And did the unbroken colt condemn arrogant people? "Christ came unto his own, and his own received him not." The beast of the field was wiser than the people who watched it. See Zechariah 9:9.

Unique in His Passion. " *A new sepulchre, wherein was never man yet laid*"

"Then took they the body of Jesus, and wound it in linen clothes with the spices, as the manner of the Jews is to bury. Now in the place where he was crucified there was a garden; and in the garden a new sepulchre, wherein *was never man yet laid*. There laid they Jesus therefore because of the Jews' preparation day; for the sepulchre was nigh at hand" (John 19:40-42). Thus was Isaiah's prophecy fulfilled. Seven centuries before the coming of Christ, he had foretold, "And he made his grave with the wicked, and with the rich in his death" (Isa. 53:9). Nicodemus and Joseph gently laid to rest the body of their Master, and quietly went home. No other had ever lain there; no other had died as He died. Christ was unique in all His preaching; He was unique in all His actions; He was unique in death. He came to give to us His message, His power, His love. He was, and is, the incomparable Christ. "The chiefest among ten thousand ... he is altogether lovely" (Song of Solomon 5:10-16).

> Wonderful, wonderful Jesus,
>   Who can compare with thee?
> Wonderful, wonderful Jesus,
>   Fairer than all art thou to me.
>
> Wonderful, wonderful Jesus,
>   Oh, how my soul loves thee:
> Fairer than all the fairest,
>   Jesus, art thou to me.

THE APOSTLES ... and the life more abundant
(JOHN 10: 10; ROMANS 5: 17; 2 CORINTHIANS 8: 12;
2 PETER 1: 11)

Regeneration, wonderful as the experience might be, is but the introduction to God's great world of truth. As birth must be followed by growth, so conversion must be followed and superseded by holiness. "That we henceforth be *no more children*. . . . But speaking the truth in love, *may grow up* into him in all things" (Eph. 4:14, 15). The systematic teaching of the New Testament has much to reveal concerning this glorious theme.

An Abundant Life

The Lord Jesus said, ". . . I am come that they might have life, *and that they might have it more abundantly*." Eternal life is the priceless gift which reaches the sinner through personal faith in the Lord Jesus Christ. Language cannot express the inestimable worth of this eternal treasure, but we do well to remember that *life abundant* is to *life* what a reservoir is to a pool. A drink of cool, refreshing water may revive a thirsty traveller, but it cannot satisfy all the requirements of his future. Eternal life brings to man a taste of the reviving springs of God's unfailing supplies, but the Lord Jesus never promised that this experience alone would meet the Christian's every need. He planned to make it possible for heaven's limitless supplies to flood human souls; that daily needs should be supplied by the inflow of divine sufficiency.

An Abundant Grace

The apostle Paul wrote, ". . . they which receive abundance of grace . . . shall reign in life by one, Jesus Christ." It will be immediately recognized that Paul's statement introduces a theme of great import. Conversion—the receiving of eternal life—introduces the believer to a spiritual kingdom. This new experience takes him to a place of power within the kingdom. "They shall *reign* in life." As the late Dr. Campbell Morgan said, "They shall trample under foot the very powers by which they were overcome." Inbred sin would be defeated by this spiritual conqueror who received abundance of grace from God. It might be helpful to link another text with this verse. "Let us therefore come boldly unto the throne of grace, that we may obtain mercy, and find grace to help in every time of need" (Heb. 4:16). Abundance of life and grace is impossible unless we commune with God.

An Abundant Joy

"... the grace of God bestowed on the churches of Macedonia; How that in a great trial of affliction the abundance of their joy and their deep poverty abounded unto the riches of their liberality." This presents a delightful study in extremes. Affliction and joy, poverty and liberality, are brought together as though they belonged to each other. Indeed, this is the case, for when a man has advanced into the realms of abundant blessing, he proves in daily experience that all things are made to work together for his good. He joyfully exclaims, "I have learned in whatsoever state I am, therein to be content." Affliction is but the sombre setting against which the scintillating jewel of joy is displayed. Deep poverty encourages faith to be increasingly active, and man reaches forth unto the inexhaustible riches of Christ, and rejoices in sacrificial giving. If we may be permitted to change the simile, let us say that abundant life is the fertile soil; abundant grace is the healthy plant; abundant joy is the radiant bloom which sends forth its fragrance to attract and enchant all who come within its domain.

An Abundant Entrance

The apostle Peter supplies the glorious climax to this stimulating study. He says in his second epistle, "... brethren, give diligence to make your calling and election sure: for if ye do these things, ye shall never fall: For so an entrance shall be ministered unto you abundantly into the everlasting kingdom of our Lord and Saviour Jesus Christ." *An abundant entrance.* Let us compare an ordinary citizen returning to his home after a brief holiday, with the national hero returning from a far country. The one man returns unnoticed; the other is awaited by excited, cheering crowds. The one man is forgotten; the other is given the freedom of the city. Both men obtain an entrance, but the one is given an abundant entrance. Are we justified in assuming that something of the sort happens in heaven? All believers obtain an entrance, for Christian citizenship is registered in the holy city. Yet the King will be waiting for certain saints in order to say, "Well done, thou good and faithful servant." Perhaps the angels will line the streets of gold, and the redeemed will sing the songs of the Homeland. Perhaps our loved ones already there will accompany us to the palace of the King. Surely these are the features of an abundant entrance. It can be ours if we gain distinction in the battles of life.

THE GOOD SHEPHERD ... and a wonderful promise

(JOHN 10: 27-29)

The shepherds and their flocks had come to the river, and while the men sat discussing their various problems, their fleecy charges jostled each other around the sparkling water. Eventually the calls of the shepherd echoed across the countryside, and immediately each flock obediently followed its master. Westerners find it hard to believe that a shepherd's voice can attract sheep from a surging collection of animals at a river bank, but such is the way of the East. The disciples probably smiled when their Master said, "I am the good Shepherd. ... My sheep hear my voice, and I know them, and they follow me: And I give unto them eternal life; and they shall never perish, neither shall any man pluck them out of my hand. My Father, which gave them me, is greater than all; and no man is able to pluck them out of my Father's hand." There is reason to believe that this was one of the Lord's greatest messages.

God's Great Grace

It is almost incomprehensible that sinners should be able to obtain a place among the followers of Christ. It has been said that a sheep is the only animal incapable of finding its way home. There may be exceptions to this rule, but it is undeniable that the innate characteristic of sheep is to wander. Perhaps Isaiah had this in mind when he said, "All we like sheep have gone astray; we have turned every one to his own way..." (Isa. 53:6). Yet the entire scene is changed when affection born of knowledge links the sheep with a shepherd. Instead of straying, the sheep are drawn irresistibly after the one who cares for them. Such is the power of grace. Straying sinners are united to the Good Shepherd by the bonds of love, and His voice is sufficient to attract them from places of danger. He said, "My sheep hear my voice ... and they follow me."

God's Great Grip

"And I give unto them eternal life, and they shall *never* perish, neither shall any man pluck them out of my hand." We do well to remember that eternal life is *eternal life*. When a man becomes a child of God, he becomes one for ever. If the priceless treasure only lasts one month, it can hardly be eternal. A son may decide to change his name, but nothing can alter the fact that he remains the child of his parent. The father may be very grieved with the actions of his son, but nothing can change affinity of nature. Thus God's transmission of life to the soul is something accomplished eternally. We may lose our grip on God, but He never loses His grip on us. "No man can pluck them out of my Father's hand." And if any further evidence were needed to justify this statement, then 1 Corinthians 5:1-5 would be sufficient. There Paul speaks of the worst backslider known to the Church. His sin was inexcusable and unprecedented. His evil influence had been so spread abroad that the apostle could not pray for his restoration. In so many words, Paul said, "Let him die; then men will forget what has happened." ". . . deliver such an one unto Satan, for the destruction of the flesh, *that the spirit may be saved* in the day of the Lord Jesus." This poor prodigal was as much his Father's son when he was filthy in the far country as when he was clean at home. Alas, he had lost everything except his soul!

God's Great Glory

God has never broken a covenant promise. His honour is at stake in the strict observance of every undertaking. Charles Haddon Spurgeon is reputed to have said, "If there were one soul in hell upon whom were the marks of the precious blood of Christ, all heaven would be away to the rescue." The doctrines of eternal security do not provide licence for sin. The reality of individual salvation is expressed in loyalty to Christ. If a man loves the Lord, he will endeavour to keep His commandments. The new birth entails more than conformity to Church law; it is far more than identification with any particular body of worshippers. It is union with Christ. No man can be united to Christ, and not wish to follow Him fully. "My sheep hear my voice, *and they follow me.*" Such people are safe in the keeping of God, and can never be lost!

> My name from the palms of His hands
>   Eternity will not erase:
> Impressed on His heart it remains,
>   In marks of indelible grace.
>
> And I to the end shall endure,
>   As sure as the earnest is given;
> More happy, but not more secure,
>   When glorified with Him in heaven.

CHRIST . . . and three out-of-season fruits
(JOHN 14: 27; 15: 11)

Out-of-season fruit is always a rare commodity. Strawberries in winter, or blackberries in the spring, will always excite comment; and if prices are not prohibitive, these rarities will always sell. Among the many fruits of the Spirit are love, joy, and peace; but sometimes these have been produced in the most unlikely places at the most unexpected time. Their appearance promotes wonder; their existence under certain conditions creates amazement. It was this fact which astonished the early Church; they had seen luscious summer fruit in winter. When icy winds had blown upon their Lord; when pre-Calvary conditions had overwhelmed all else with dreariness and woe, the very choicest of heaven's fruit had been found in the words and actions of the Saviour.

My Peace

"Peace I leave with you, my peace I give unto you; not as the world giveth, give I unto you. Let not your heart be troubled, neither let it be afraid" (John 14:27). It seemed incongruous for Christ to speak about His peace when men were planning to murder Him. Treachery of the worst type was about to be exhibited, and even the disciples were soon to demonstrate their unfaithfulness. Alone, and in pain, the Lord had every reason to feel bitterness of soul rather than to speak serenely of His undisturbed tranquillity. "My peace I give unto you." Anxiety was firmly banished from His mind; hatred did not exist in His heart. Assured that all was well, He calmly walked with God. His soul was an ocean of divine compassion, unruffled by malice; a place of abiding restfulness.

My Love

"As the Father hath loved me, so have I loved you: continue ye in my love" (John 15:9). Constantly the Lord had been challenged by frustration and disappointment. The Pharisees hated Him; the self-confident disciples were about to forsake Him; and Judas would soon sell his loyalty for pieces of silver. Could any tree produce the fruit of love in face of such biting winds of evil? Could Christ endure such detestable conditions, and at the same time preserve the sweet purity of His spirit? Could love overcome hatred even as peace overcame anxiety? Where sin abounded, grace much more abounded. Christ loved them all—even Judas; and the words spoken on that occasion seem now to be rays of brilliance shining from an ancient lighthouse. From the blackness of the past, the light shines forth to guide us safely into the harbour of the divine will. Christ said, " If I have loved you, ye ought also to love one another." A Christian whose love exists only in his theology is a tinkling cymbal; a sound without music; a desert without life.

My Joy

"These things have I spoken unto you, that my joy might remain in you, and that your joy might be full " (John 15:11). " The fruit of the spirit is . . . joy." Calvary's horizon had already appeared dark and ominous; the spikes destined to draw blood from the Master's body had already been forged. The gibbet was already lying in some timber yard awaiting the command which would take it forth to carry its precious burden. Apparently everything had gone wrong with God's world, and the road to the green hill was ready for the blood which would stain its dust. Christ knew that His hour had come, and calmly welcomed the end. Did I say " the end "? I was wrong. Let the readers accept my apologies. Christ went forth to meet His death knowing it would be a tunnel leading to a new era. At the end of the last supper he had announced a hymn, and probably pitched the tune. Emotion almost prevented the disciples from singing their parts, but His resonant, wonderful voice re-echoed the music of His soul. They wondered how He could be so buoyant and serene when everything had gone against Him. Whence came the charm of His manner, the rich cadence of His tone, the supreme confidence of His bearing? Was He not to be crucified? Alas, the disciples were short-sighted. They saw the cross; He saw the throne. " . . . Let us run with patience the race that is set before us, Looking unto Jesus . . . who for the *joy* that was set before him endured the cross, despising the shame, and is set down at the right hand of God " (Heb. 12:2). His joy overcame sadness, pain, and death, and secured a deep content which defied the terrors of crucifixion. This joy He desired to share with His followers. He said, " . . . that my joy might remain in you, and that your joy might be full."

Love, joy, peace! These were summer fruits produced in winter. They were rare, and very costly.

CHRIST . . . and His tantalizing inconsistency
(John 18: 4-8)

It was not always easy to understand the actions and teachings of the Lord Jesus, and there were many occasions when the disciples were nonplussed. Extreme weariness was evident when He lay asleep in the storm-tossed boat, yet within minutes, omnipotence hushed the raging seas. At one moment the disciples felt they had a very human brother and leader; the next they gasped with astonishment and cried, "What manner of man is this?" The strangest contrast of this kind is found in John's Gospel.

An Unexpected Collapse

The silence of the garden had been rudely shattered by the excited clamouring of a fanatical mob. Led by the traitor Judas, the people had come to arrest the Nazarene. There was to be no mistake this time! Feelings of antagonism had been roused to intensity; the meddlesome Carpenter was to be removed before Passover. Like hunting dogs eager for the kill, the rabble pressed forward as their lanterns turned the garden into a bewitched fairyland. "Jesus therefore, knowing all things which should come upon him, went forth, and said unto them, Whom seek ye? They answered him, Jesus of Nazareth. Jesus saith unto them, I *am*. And Judas also, which betrayed him, stood with them. As soon then as he had said unto them, *I am*, they went backward and fell to the ground." And amid all the astounding events of that dread week, this surely must rank as the greatest. It was distractingly humiliating to have one's face pressed into the dust before Him whom they desired to capture. How easy it is to believe that when Christ shall be manifested in glory, every knee will bow, and every tongue will confess that He is Lord.

A Unique Challenge

What was the cause of this amazing collapse? There can only be one answer. Invisible power; irresistible dynamic swept them off their feet when Jesus said, *I am*. It will be seen that the word "he" has been printed in italics. It was placed there by the translators in order—as they thought—to make the passage readable. They erred, for the Scripture would have been its own interpreter. I AM is God's name. When Moses asked the Lord, saying, ". . . when I come unto the children of Israel, and shall say unto them, The God of your fathers hath sent me unto you; and they shall say to me, What is his name? what shall I say unto them?" God answered him, saying, "I AM THAT I AM: and he said, Thus shalt thou say unto the children of Israel, I AM hath sent me unto you" (Exod. 3:13, 14). God is the eternally present; and this was the name given by Christ in the garden of Gethsemane. It represented His claim to deity; and the power which overcame the crowd more than endorsed the words of His great challenge.

An Unopposed Coup

When His question was repeated, the dazed men slowly regained their feet, and hesitantly answered that they sought the Nazarene. Within a few minutes they were binding the Lord Jesus with ropes brought specially for the job; but the arrogance of some of those men had been severely jolted. It was unnatural for omnipotence to be overcome by men who only minutes before had been paralysed by two of His words. The confused scene needs an explanation. If the disciples ran for their lives, at least we can appreciate their stupefaction when they saw their glorious leader submitting in such a perplexing manner. We sympathize with Simon Peter, whose impetuosity severed the ear of Malchus. The Master's quiet rebuke demoralized His followers, and feeling the cause was lost, they turned to flee. The mob took Jesus away, and even the angels wept—or did they? Perhaps they were too amazed.

An Undisguised Concern

Some things stand out in bold relief. It is quite obvious that had Christ desired to resist aggression, He could easily have done so. That He permitted the enemies to lead Him away suggests that He preferred to go with them. Yet before He finally capitulated, the Lord made a request which was instantly granted. "If therefore ye seek me, *let these go their way*." In that grim hour of danger, He sacrificed Himself that His followers might be protected. "Having loved His own . . . He loved them unto the end." It is not too much to say that Christ's intercession saved the men who thought He had failed them. What would the savage crowd have done to Simon Peter when one of their comrades stood disfigured and bleeding? "He ever liveth to make intercession for us." It was true then—it is true now. What a wonderful Saviour!

TWO MEN ... who triumphed in the end
(JOHN 19: 38-42)

The scene was dark and sombre, for men had done their worst: Jesus was dead. The longings aroused in multitudes of hearts had perished, and the fairest Messianic hope in centuries had petered out. Alone, and friendless, the Carpenter had been crucified; and His enemies were jubilant. Wrapped in the shadows of the green hill, the ugly cross seemed sinister and hateful; a thing to be shunned in a locality to be avoided. And then suddenly a man approached. His movements were eerie; his presence frightening. He paused to listen. Someone else was coming: Footfalls echoed through the silence. "And there came also Nicodemus, which at the first came to Jesus by night, and brought a mixture of myrrh and aloes, about an hundred pound weight. Then took they the body of Jesus, and wound it in linen clothes with the spices, as the manner of the Jews is to bury. Now in the place where he was crucified, there was a garden; and in the garden a new sepulchre, wherein was never man yet laid. There laid they Jesus therefore because of the Jews' preparation day; for the sepulchre was nigh at hand." The funeral was over; the two men stood before the tomb. They had known a long, grim struggle; and although they had suffered many setbacks, their courage had ultimately triumphed gloriously. Even the angels were smiling.

Their Great Confidence

Nicodemus and Joseph had one thing in common—they looked for the Messiah. It would appear that whereas the ruler of the synagogue was governed by intellect, Joseph of Arimathea was ruled by his heart. One man was pre-eminently a thinker—the teacher of Israel; the other was an honourable counsellor, of whom all men spoke well. We know that the teacher visited Christ under cover of darkness. Probably aware that Daniel had foretold the time of Messiah's coming, and that the stipulated time had already elapsed, Nicodemus wanted to know if Jesus of Nazareth were the Messiah. Thus he planned his night visit (John 3). We do not know how Joseph first made contact with Christ. Possibly he stood on the edge of a crowd and heard the greatest sermon of his life. He saw also the sick being healed, and his doubts were instantly dispelled. Confidence was born in the hearts of both men, yet neither of them had the courage to make open confession of his faith. Nicodemus carefully preserved the secret of his visit to Jesus; and of Joseph, the Scriptures declare that he was "a disciple of Jesus, but secretly for fear of the Jews" (John 19:38).

Their Great Cowardice

Let us not condemn these men; they had many difficulties to overcome. On one occasion at least Nicodemus made an attempt to support Christ. When the conference chamber was in an uproar; when the Sanhedrin was incensed because the officers of the law had failed to bring in their prisoner; when tempers were frayed, and anger threatened violence, "Nicodemus saith unto them. . . . Doth our law judge any man, before it hear him, and know what he doeth? They answered and saith unto him, Art thou also of Galilee? Search, and look: for out of Galilee ariseth no prophet" (John 7:50-52). Nicodemus remained silent. His intellectual capabilities might have provided a glorious defence for Jesus, but rather than risk the animosity of his fellow rulers, he withdrew into obscurity. At a later meeting, when the council decided to crucify the Lord, "Joseph did not consent to their deed." He hated the decision of his fellow counsellors, but decided that discretion was the better part of valour. There were others who similarly remained silent (John 12:42, 43).

Their Great Conquest

It was all over; they had lost their chance to kneel before a living Christ. Joseph, haunted by memories, and ashamed of his earlier cowardice, decided to do the only decent thing left to do. He made himself responsible for the funeral of his Lord. In another part of the city, Nicodemus, driven by remorse, and utterly ashamed of his unworthiness, determined upon a similar course of action. It seemed a thousand pities that he was unable to confess his faith before Christ, but at least he could be true to his memory. These courageous men met before the cross, and redeeming love united their hearts. We do well to remember that neither man expected the resurrection. Their immediate outlook was one which envisaged persecution and ribaldry. The victorious Sanhedrin would not be silent in regard to this burial. Their sneers would mean abuse. Fully aware of the coming storm, the two disciples determined to atone for the years of fear when cowardice had ruined their testimony. They went forth to bury a dead Christ, and soon rejoiced in the fellowship of a risen Saviour. Some day we may have the chance to ask what the Lord said to them when they met. How proud they would be to hear, "Well done, thou good and faithful servants."

PETER . . . who was told to mind his own business
(JOHN 21: 21-22)

The nature of Simon Peter might have been described under three heads—(i) *He was very impulsive.* His fellow disciples hardly knew what to expect from this big fisherman, for while they soberly considered the pros and cons of a matter, their colleague enthusiastically pronounced a verdict. (ii) *He was very inquisitive.* He was susceptible to the opinions of other people, and more often than not this led to trouble. (iii) *He was very inflammable,* very temperamental. He could be alternately joyful and sad; inspired and carnal. Yet in spite of that fact, we all like Simon Peter.

A Dangerous Concern

The sea-side breakfast had ended, and the disciples were watching the silvery waves moving along the beach. Surging emotions filled their souls, for they realized that the Stranger who had awaited the incoming boat was the Lord. It was wonderful to see Him as He gracefully sat watching the hungry men eating the meal He Himself had prepared. Tenderly He had spoken to Peter, and the thrice-asked question, "Lovest thou me," had stirred them deeply. Their colleague had been moved almost to tears, for the denials of an earlier occasion were still present in his mind. Then, after a while Peter looked at John and said to Christ, "Lord, and what shall this man do?" "You tell me that when I am old another shall gird me and carry me whither I would not. Well, what about John? What will happen to him?" And the Lord answered, "If I will that he tarry till I come, what is that to thee?" Simon Peter, your greatest mistake is that you are often looking at, and thinking of, other people. Do you remember how I sent you to take money from the mouth of the fish? You were upset then because other people's opinions had overshadowed your outlook. Do you remember how you denied knowledge of me? That happened because you permitted other people to influence you. Peter, be less concerned about other folk, and think more of your Master!

A Delightful Correction

"What is that to thee?" "If I be the Lord, and you are My servant, your chief aim should be to do My will. If I decide that John should linger till I return, that is no business of yours, is it? Simon Peter, if you are to feed My lambs, and shepherd My sheep, you will need to look constantly to

Me. The days ahead will be difficult, and if you lose sight of your Master anything can happen. Therefore do not be unduly inquisitive concerning John. Attend to your own affairs." Thus did Christ correct His disciple, and we all realize how necessary this had become. Even in after days Simon still permitted the opinions of others to sway his actions, and on one occasion Paul rebuked him because he compromised with the exponents of circumcision. Peter was always getting into trouble because he had not mastered the art of minding his own business.

A Definite Command

"Follow thou me." When Peter heard this command, his thoughts probably went back to the morning when the Lord first called him, when after borrowing Peter's boat, Christ said, "Follow me, and I will make you to become a fisher of men." Now another commission has been given. He has been told to shepherd the flock of God. "Simon follow Me, for only thus will you succeed." (i) *The Follow Me of Enlightenment.* The Christian pathway is beset with many dangers, and problems will arise to confound those who are not prepared for the emergencies of the way. Follow Me, and you will learn of Me. (ii) *The Follow Me of Endeavour.* To follow Christ means to emulate His example. It means more than accompanying Him. When a soldier follows an officer into battle, he does so to help his leader in the conflict ahead. To follow Christ means to fight for Him. (iii) *The Follow Me of Endurance.* "But when thou shalt be old, thou shalt stretch forth thy hands, and another shall gird thee, and carry thee whither thou wouldest not. This spake he, signifying by what death he should glorify God." Tradition asserts that Peter was crucified for his faith; and that at his own request he was crucified head downwards, for he considered himself unworthy to die as did his Lord. Thus the fearful disciple who failed before the taunts of a servant girl, eventually reached unprecedented heights of personal loyalty. He followed his Lord to a cross; he was faithful unto death.

THE CHURCH . . . and the first Seventh Day Adventists

(ACTS 15: 1-19)

"And certain men which came down from Judæa taught the brethren, and said, Except ye be circumcised after the manner of Moses, ye cannot be saved. When therefore Paul and Barnabas had no small dissension and disputation with them, they determined that Paul and Barnabas, and certain other of them, should go up to Jerusalem unto the apostles and elders about this question."

The Church Disturbed

"And when they were come to Jerusalem, they were received of the church . . . and they declared all things that God had done with them. But there rose up certain of the sect of the Pharisees which believed, saying, That it was needful to circumcise them, and to command them to keep the law of Moses. And the apostles and elders came together for to consider of this matter." The first Church Council handled one of the most controversial points in doctrine. Let it be said in all fairness that these advocates of Moses were believers, and there is every reason to say they were utterly sincere. They could not reconcile this new freedom with the age-old practice of keeping the law. Liberty could lead to licence, and it was incumbent upon all Christians to maintain the standards of moral and spiritual law as outlined by the patriarch. Gentile converts should be circumcised, and reminded of their obligation to honour God's word. Faith was wonderful, but faith without works was dead. The chief value of Christ lay in the fact that He would enable man to keep the law—a thing which in his own strength man would never be able to do. When the apostles heard these views, they realized that a problem of major importance had arisen to threaten the unity of the Church.

The Church Discerning

The meeting was far from quiet; feelings and exchanges were animated. "And when there had been much disputing, Peter rose up, and said unto them, Men and brethren, ye know how that a good while ago God made choice among us, that the Gentiles by my mouth should hear the word of the gospel, and believe. And God, which knoweth the hearts, bare them witness, giving them the Holy Ghost, even as he did unto us; *And put no difference between us and them,* purifying their hearts by faith. Now therefore why tempt ye God, to put a yoke upon the neck of the disciples, which neither our fathers nor we were able to bear." When Peter's opinion was endorsed by James, and when as Chairman of the meeting he said, " My sentence is, that we trouble not them, which from among the Gentiles are turned to God," it became obvious that the Church had decided one of the greatest issues ever to challenge her authority. Converts were to avoid giving unnecessary offence to unbelievers; but having done that, they were freed from circumcision requirements, and were not obliged to conform to this part of Mosaic law. The Church had discerned that " the law was a schoolmaster to bring us to Christ "; that since the death of Christ had fulfilled every demand of Moses, in Him mankind had been freed from legal slavery. This great decision was written by the scribes, and sent to all the churches; and while many people refused to accept the ruling, the apostles nevertheless had clearly stated what in their opinion was the mind of Christ.

The Church Deciding

This decision led to outstanding changes in the practice of the early Christians. From time immemorial the religious services had been held on the Sabbath, but now the old order was rejected. In after days, Paul often entered into the synagogue on the Sabbath day, because such an assembly provided an opportunity for him to preach. But when the Christians met together, they chose the first day of the week— the day of resurrection (Acts 20:7). There is no record of any Christian meeting in New Testament days being held on the seventh day. There is no record of any inspired message commanding the Christians to observe and keep the law of Moses. Modern teachers might suggest that the apostles made a mistake; that they went out of the will of God; that they sinned in leading the Church astray. Yet if this were the case, the same teachers must explain how God blessed these misguided men, and used their ministry to evangelize a lost world. I have met the most charming Christians among Seventh Day Adventists, and I readily admit that their company has been a sheer delight. I have met others of the same faith whose charm has been less conspicuous. Their desire to keep the Sabbath —and to make all others do likewise—has been extremely fanatical. It is not enough to keep the Sabbath day holy. True Christians will keep *every* day holy, for in the sight of God Wednesday holiness is as necessary as Sabbath holiness.

PAUL AND BARNABAS ... whom we invite to a debate

(ACTS 15: 37-40)

Dear Brethren,

The story of your quarrel reminds us of an old query—What happens when an irresistible force meets an immovable object? We are intensely sorry that your fellowship was marred by the bitterness of a quarrel, for we feel your discord could have been avoided. Yet, brethren, we are strangely attracted by your difference of opinion, and we feel constrained to ask you to state your case. If we are able to understand the pros and cons of the matter, we shall appreciate the reasons for your actions. Barnabas, we have always liked you. Please explain to us your position in regard to this difference of opinion.

A Great Tenderness

" Brethren, I don't know that I'm glad to respond to your invitation, for these things are best forgotten. You want to know why I desired to give John Mark another chance. Does God cast us off for ever when we make mistakes? Did Christ refuse to take Simon Peter back? Did the Eternal Father and the Eternal Son quarrel over the matter of His restoration? No. God's love is greater than man's sin. Indeed, I would like to ask my brother Paul if he ever failed, and whether or not the Lord refused to reinstate him. Of course, John Mark had let us all down; but he was only a child, and Paul's own doctrine says, ' Brethren, if a man be overtaken in a fault, ye which are spiritual, restore such an one in the spirit of meekness; considering thyself, lest thou also be tempted ' (Gal. 6:1). My brother's action condemned the boy in the eyes of all the Church. Paul himself had committed far worse crimes, and who was he to refuse to overlook the faults of a mere boy?" Thank you, Barnabas. You will not mind if we reserve judgment. There are always two sides to a picture, and now Paul will give us his side.

A Great Testimony

"Barnabas, my brother still, and brethren. There is much truth in all that has been spoken. In the final analysis, I should be the last person in the world to accuse anyone of unfaithfulness. I, who was a murderer and a persecutor of the faith, should always be willing to grant mercy to others. And indeed I am; only circumstances alter cases. Our Lord had died to redeem us, and it was with His great commission

(B) *This part of the lesson poses a serious problem: How are differences between personnel in the Christian Cause to be resolved without doing harm to the ongoing work of the Church?*

that we went forth into the unknown. Our standards of efficiency were provided by Christ Himself. He declared that if a man once put his hand to the plough and looked back, he was unfit for the kingdom. John Mark deserted his duty, his commission, his friends, for the one purpose of returning to his mother and his home. Supposing our Lord had acted similarly when the anguish of Gethsemane brought blood from His temples. No. How could we expect unbelievers to accept our message when weakness was manifest in the missionaries? Indeed, I was kind to John Mark. I prevented an even greater tragedy, for if he failed in the least of his troubles, what would he have done later? I did my duty to Christ and the Church, and the fact that I received the recommendation of the brethren proves my case."

Human frailty will always make itself evident, but it concerns he kept at a minimum by much prayer & wise leadership.

A Great Tragedy

Brethren, you are waiting to hear our findings. What shall we say? Surely you were both right, and you were both wrong. The fire in your hearts reached your heads—and that is always dangerous. John Mark was never meant to be a preacher, and you, Barnabas, made a mistake in trying to fit a round peg into a square hole. John Mark was destined to sit at a desk, to collect the facts which in after days were to thrill a world. Mark was never fitted to become a pioneer missionary. Barnabas, you allowed sentiment to blind your eyes to this obvious fact. And you, Paul, must share the blame, for you also had earlier encouraged the young man. You were quite right about the wisdom of not taking him the second time; but oh, brother, that wretched quarrel! And you, Barnabas, were right in helping the boy; but when you persisted in the effort to make him a preacher, you merely walked into obscurity. If only you two fellows had held a lengthy prayer meeting first, your business meeting would have been happier. Mark was meant to fill another niche in the plans of God, and if you had paused to consider the matter, your mutual aid would have placed Mark on the road to success. Barnabas, we are so sorry that you disappeared from the sacred record. Paul, we are glad that in the end you sent for Mark, recognizing that he was profitable to you in the Gospel. Well done, both of you; but you were foolish to quarrel—weren't you?

(A) *One author gives us this thought in regard to John Mark — "Barnabus's encouragement & Paul's sharp tones made a man of Mark — as later we find him helping Paul.*

PAUL . . . who left the mainspring out of his watch

(ACTS 17: 16-34)

"Now while Paul waited . . . at Athens, his spirit was stirred in him, when he saw the city wholly given to idolatry." A dreamy indolence pervaded the streets, for when its citizens were not prostrating themselves before their idols, they gathered to debate new doctrines. Paul stood before the images, read the inscriptions, and turned away sickened when deluded people placed offerings at the feet of a god who could neither see nor appreciate what was being done. He moved along the street, and seeing yet another of these Athenian gods, paused to read its inscription. When he saw "To the Unknown God," his eyes became stars, and his grim face softened. So, after all, these people believed there might be another God. "And Paul's spirit was stirred in him."

An Intense Desire

"Therefore disputed he in the synagogue with the Jews, and with the devout persons, and in the market place daily with them that met with him." Probably he challenged his compatriots with the fact that their silence was inexcusable. Why were they not upholding the faith of the fathers, and denouncing idolatry? From the synagogue he went into the market place, and his open-air meetings became a feature of the city. "Then certain philosophers of the Epicureans, and of the Stoicks, encountered him. And some said, What will this babbler say? Others said, He seemeth to be a setter forth of strange gods: because he preached unto them Jesus and the resurrection. And they took him, and brought him unto Areopagus, saying, May we know what this new doctrine, whereof thou speakest, is?" And thus Paul was presented with his supreme opportunity in Athens.

An Interesting Discourse

"Then Paul stood in the midst of Mars' hill, and said, Ye men of Athens, I perceive that in all things ye are too superstitious. For as I passed by, and beheld your devotions, I found an altar with this inscription, TO THE UNKNOWN GOD. Whom then ye ignorantly worship, him declare I unto you." And the oration which followed was easily one of the best of Paul's speeches. A great psychologist, he correctly read the thoughts of his audience; and quoting their own poets, he logically reasoned concerning the greatest things in religion. Yet he omitted one detail. If we are to judge by this record, he did not mention the name of Jesus. He merely referred to Him as "*that man.*" He realized that the cross would be foolishness to his intellectual audience, and avoided all mention of the death of Christ. He preached a Christ without a Cross; a risen Lord but no redemption; the certainty of judgment but no explanation of how a man may be justified. This was a glorious oration, but somehow it didn't work—he had left the mainspring out of his watch.

An Increasing Dissatisfaction

"And when they heard of the resurrection of the dead, some mocked: and others said, We will hear thee again of this matter. So Paul departed from among them." And in after days, Paul had plenty of time to reflect upon his message. He was not satisfied. He had reasoned with the Athenians; he had been an expert psychologist; but "the foolishness of God is wiser than men." These absurd doctrines of reconciliation through the death of Christ had the uncanny knack of transforming lives. These apparent absurdities completely changed the outlook of human beings. Apparently the meeting on Mars' hill had been a great success; his oratory had delighted his hearers; *but he had not founded a Church.* He never did this in Athens.

An Illuminating Decision

"After these things Paul departed from Athens, and came to Corinth. . . ." And even as he journeyed, regret nagged at his peace of mind; frustration tormented his great longings, and out of his surging emotions came a fierce resolve. He would know nothing among men but Jesus Christ and Him crucified. Soon, the people of Corinth were hearing of the death of Christ; and within a short time, a Christian Church was established in the city. Long afterward Paul referred to that first visit to Corinth. "And I, brethren, when I came to you, came not with excellency of speech or of wisdom, declaring unto you the testimony of God. For I determined not to know anything among you, save Jesus Christ, and him crucified" (1 Cor. 2:1, 2). A watch without a mainspring is dead mechanism; a Gospel without a Calvary is dead dogma! Neither will work!

PAUL . . . who could be as stubborn as a mule
(ACTS 21: 4-13)

Paul was one of the greatest of all Christians. He was a man of steel, and never turned back from his duty. Possessed of unending courage, he took the Gospel to all parts of the known world; and when many contemporaries failed, this brave missionary continued until the end of his earthly journey. Yet, as is often the case with men of his calibre, his strength was his weakness. His will power was a snare. He mistook bravery for guidance.

An Intense Desire

Paul loved his nation, and his greatest ambition was to win fellow Jews for Christ. When God called him to be the apostle to the Gentiles, the man of Tarsus could not hide his disappointment. He honestly believed he was the man to win the Jews, and even argued with God over the matter. " And it came to pass, that, when I was come again to Jerusalem, even while I prayed in the temple, I was in a trance; And saw him saying unto me, Make haste, and get thee quickly out of Jerusalem: for they will not receive thy testimony concerning me. And I said, Lord, they know that I imprisoned and beat in every synagogue them that believed on thee. . . . And he said unto me, Depart: for I will send you far hence to the Gentiles " (Acts 22: 17-21). Paul obeyed his Lord; but the synagogues always attracted him. At every opportunity he entered these buildings, to expound the word of life; and it is very problematical whether he was justified in doing this. At one time he confessed he could wish himself a castaway if only his people might be saved. This intense desire to reach Israel eventually led Paul into much trouble.

An Inspired Discernment

" . . . and we landed at Tyre: for there the ship was to unlade her burden. And finding disciples, we tarried there seven days: *who said to Paul through the Spirit, that he should not go up to Jerusalem.* And when we had accomplished those days, we departed and went our way." This was disobedience. Paul interpreted the message as having arisen from brotherly sentiment and not from the mind of God. " . . . And we came unto Cæsarea: and we entered into the house of Philip the evangelist. . . . And the same man had four daughters which did prophesy. And as we tarried there many days, there came down from Judæa a certain prophet named Agabus. . . . He took Paul's girdle, and bound his own hands and feet, and said, *Thus saith the Holy Ghost,* So shall the Jews of Jerusalem bind the man that owneth this girdle." This was God's second warning to Paul. Alas, the apostle had made up his mind to go to Jerusalem. He was as stubborn as a mule!

An Insistent Demand

Luke records, "And when we heard these things, both we, and they of that place, besought him not to go up to Jerusalem." Philip the evangelist; his four prophesying daughters; Doctor Luke, the beloved physician; and all the brethren, united to ask Paul to obey the commands of the Holy Spirit. Paul answered, "What mean ye to weep and to break mine heart? for I am ready not to be bound only, but also to die at Jerusalem for the name of the Lord Jesus. *And when he would not be persuaded, we ceased."* Paul, these were very brave words, and your sentiments were of the highest order; but to die for Christ is all wrong when God desires you to live and preach the Gospel. The glory of a martyr's death cannot take the place of a lifetime of service. Paul, you were very unwise; but we admire your zeal nevertheless. Oh, that such devotion could be found in the hearts of all the people of God! Yet, that does not alter the fact that you were disobedient, and lost two years of valuable opportunities.

An Inexcusable Disobedience

" And after those days we took up our carriages, and went up to Jerusalem." Within a short time Paul was taken by the authorities and imprisoned, and for the agonizing period of two years he could only think of the vast opportunities which had been lost. Instead of sitting on a prison bench, he could have been telling the glorious Gospel message in the market places of Asia. We know that God over-ruled in these matters; but the truth remains that Paul's stubbornness robbed him of many chances to spread further the kingdom of Christ. And all this goes to prove that God's way is better than ours. Sometimes we need more courage to deny self than we need to go to prison, and even Paul would agree that it is far better to be leading souls to Christ than to languish unnecessarily in a dungeon.

PAUL... who proved it's an ill wind that blows no good

(ACTS 28: 1)

It has often been said that life is like a carpet. When viewed from the wrong side, the pattern is fantastic and meaningless; when seen from the correct side, the same colourful threads produce perfection and design. Life's experiences may be horribly disconcerting, but we have reason to believe that ultimately we shall understand how God makes all things work together for good to them that love Him. Our side of life's carpet may be confusing; let us believe that God is too wise to make mistakes. Luke supplies a wonderful example of this fact.

A Saviour Discerning

Far out in the Mediterranean Sea lay the small island of Melita. It represented a world of its own, for few were the contacts made with the rest of civilization. Trading ships occasionally visited the small harbour, but apart from these connections the islanders had little association with other people. The chief man was named Publius, and at the time of this story his father was dangerously ill. Probably hæmorrhages had drained the older man's energies and undermined his resistance to disease. The stricken family were so far removed from the necessary medical assistance that death seemed inevitable. The people were heathen, and had no spiritual realities upon which to lean in their time of need. The position was desperate; but the Lord was not unmindful of His people. He saw, He understood, and He cared.

A Storm Diverting

Away to the East a sailing ship, well behind schedule, slowly made its way toward Phenice, where the captain and the crew expected to winter. It appeared that nothing could prevent the fulfilment of their plans, for even the winds were favourable (Acts 27:13). Yet aboard that vessel was Paul, whose presence was urgently required on the distant island. There was no other servant of God who could move into the emergency, and unless supernatural powers intervened, even Paul would fail to reach Melita in time. The Lord decided to take a hand in affairs. "Not long afterward there arose ... a tempestuous wind, called Euroclydon. And when the ship was caught, and could not bear up into the wind, we let her drive." It was then that the unseen Pilot took charge. With unerring accuracy the vessel was driven from its usual course, and although it took a considerable time to bring the missionary to the desired haven, ultimately the devastating storm achieved this purpose.

A Saint Dispensing

"And it came to pass, that the father of Publius lay sick with a fever and a bloody flux: to whom Paul entered in, and prayed, and laid hands on him, and healed him. So when this was done, others also, which had diseases in the island, came, and were healed" (Acts 28:8, 9). And since Paul remained in the island for three months, it may be safely assumed that he often preached the Gospel. His unexpected appearance had been providential, and Church history proves that his ministry to the islanders was not in vain. It is also noteworthy that Doctor Luke was one of Paul's companions. God's healing powers do not abolish the necessity for the exercise of wisdom. We have a part to play in the fulfilment of the divine purpose. Miraculous power was given to Paul, who in Christ's name dispensed it to needy people. He was a true missionary.

A Suggestion Disclosing

Long afterward Paul wrote, "And we know that all things work together for good to them that love God, to them who are the called according to his purpose" (Rom. 8:28). The apostle had many experiences which suggested this fact, yet the storm which took him to Melita was perhaps the greatest. Discomfort, depression, and danger had all appeared in the strange pattern of those frightening days; but God's hand was at work, and it was His wisdom which directed the course of the storm-tossed ship. Everything was perfectly in order, for God was over-ruling in the affairs of men. And since God is unchanging, we may be assured the same providence over-rules our affairs. Stormy circumstances may buffet the soul; disaster may appear to overwhelm us; but when Christ is our pilot we are safe.

> Simply trusting every day,
> Trusting, through a stormy way;
> Even when my faith is small,
> Trusting Jesus, that is all.

PAUL ... and the greatness of God's salvation
(ROMANS 5: 10)

"For if, when we were enemies, we were reconciled to God by the death of his Son, much more, being reconciled, we shall be saved by his life." This wonderful verse occupies an important place in the structure of the epistle. The first eight chapters of the letter expound the Gospel of God. Four chapters are devoted to the *Gospel for the sinner*; four chapters are likewise used to expound the *Gospel for the saint*. It will be recognized therefore that this expository gem comes at the end of the first section, and at the beginning of the second. It sums up the former teaching, and anticipates the latter. It seems like a mountain lodge, from which we view the shadows of the valley, and at the same time obtain glimpses of the sunlit heights whither we journey.

The Vision of the Valley

Paul uses three outstanding words to describe the position of sinful man—*sinner, slave,* and *enemy*. A sinner is a man who has violated the laws of God; one who has thereby incurred the wrath of God. A slave is one in whose heart evil has gained supremacy. The sinner has become a *helpless* sinner. An enemy is one who loves his sin, and who takes up arms in its defence. Open warfare exists between man and his Creator. This final state represents the lowest depths to which humans can sink. Against the darkness of this sombre setting, three facts shine forth as stars. (i) *God's great mercy,* "... when we were enemies"; (ii) *God's great miracle,* "we were reconciled to God"; (iii) *God's great means,* "by the death of his Son." God sent His Son to reconcile a sinful world, and this was accomplished through the sacrifice consummated at the cross of Calvary. There He died, the just for the unjust, that He might bring us to God; and this happened when we were yet in our sins, enemies, fighting against God. Yet, the reconciliation gained through the death of Christ had to be made real in the experiences of guilty men. Peace had been obtained, but only personal faith could end the state of warfare. Paul began the second section of the epistle with the words, "Therefore being justified by faith, we *have* peace with God." Thus the upward climb was commenced, and when Paul paused at his mountain lodge he was able to obtain a comprehensive view of the valley from which God's grace had rescued him. Then he turned to look upwards. Ahead lay the beckoning peaks of holiness, and swayed by the inspiration of that thrilling moment, the apostle wrote, "... much more, being reconciled, we shall be saved by his life."

The Challenge of the Summit

Unless we realize at the outset that God's salvation is infinitely more than the forgiveness of sin, the words "we shall be saved" may be misleading. There are many Christians who hold that God's children may be lost when they fall back into sin. This belief is contrary to the teaching of the Scriptures. When God saves a man, He saves him for ever. Eternal life *is* eternal life; and Christ said, "No man can pluck them out of my Father's hand." The purposes of God are not limited to man's regeneration; it is predestined that he should be "conformed to the image of God's dear Son." Christ has already lifted His people *from the uttermost*; He is determined to continue the work in lifting them *to the uttermost*. Once again the identical facts already recognized become apparent. (i) *God's great mercy*. This is "from everlasting to everlasting upon them that fear him." The mercy manifest in man's conversion, is seen again in man's continuance. Paul's irrefutable argument is expressed in two great words—*much more*. If God thought it worth while to reconcile us when we were yet sinners, enemies against God, it naturally follows that He will continue the work; for bad as we might be, we are not as bad as we were! We are no longer enemies, but sons and daughters of the Most High; we are no longer afar off, but have been made nigh by the blood of Jesus. (ii) *God's great miracle*. John wrote, "Beloved, now are we the sons of God, and it doth not yet appear what we shall be: but we know that, *when he shall appear, we shall be like him,* for we shall see him as he is" (1 John 3:2). Inherent evil will be completely overcome, and freed from the presence of sin, we shall appear before God "without blemish; without spot or wrinkle." (iii) *God's great means*. A fair translation of the final sentence would be, "We shall be saved by sharing in His life." The life of the risen Lord can be made real in the experience of the believer as the Holy Spirit comes to indwell the human temple. Indeed, He is the eternal guide who would lead us up the mountain of God.

PAUL . . . and the ministry of women
(1 Corinthians 14: 34, 35; 1 Timothy 2: 11, 12)

It is not possible to understand the commands of Paul concerning the behaviour of women in the Church until we consider the circumstances in which these words were uttered. The women of the East are never permitted to sit with their men in a service. Seldom are they permitted even to attend a mosque; and in Jewish synagogues, places are set apart where they must sit alone. Sometimes a flimsy curtain is all that divides the sexes, and the noisy chatter of uninterested females often disturbs a meeting. In certain places it is still necessary to silence the ladies in the Church. Where women are considered to be little more than slaves, it is necessary that men should propagate the Gospel message. Yet to assert that enlightened women must always be silent is neither in keeping with the Scriptures nor with common sense. Millions of souls, men and women, have been won for Christ through consecrated womanhood.

The Woman Who Prayed—1 Samuel 1: 11, 12

The opening chapters of the first book of Samuel provide a thought-provoking contrast. A woman's constancy is seen in bold relief against a background of masculine failure. Most men had miserably failed in those days of national declension, yet one woman took her petitions to the altar of God, and her prayers saved a nation. There is reason to believe that the secret of the success of the Christian Church may be traced to the power of the prayers ascending from the hearts of a great host of Christian women. All women may emulate the example of their ancient sister.

The Women Who Preached—Acts 21: 8, 9

"Philip the evangelist was one of the seven. . . . And the same man had four daughters, virgins, which did prophesy." Philip was an early Church leader, a man upon whom rested the blessing of God. It would seem that his gift had been imparted to his family, for his four daughters followed his example. We are not told where or when they exercised their ministry, but it may be assumed that they also tried to influence Paul in regard to the folly of resisting the Holy Ghost (vv. 11, 12). There is a diversity of gifts in the Church. Some people minister to the Lord in prayer, others minister for the Lord in service. Happy is that Christian, man or woman, who is privileged to tell forth the greatest message in the world. Happy, too, is that father whose influence turns a home into a sanctuary where children are taught to love and preach Christ.

The Woman Who Practised What Others Preached—Acts 9:36

" Now there was at Joppa a certain disciple named Tabitha, which by interpretation is called Dorcas: this woman was full of good works and alms which she did." Her gracious spirit and shining example of Christian charity charmed the community and enriched the Church. It was a cause for intense grief when bereavement robbed the fellowship of this outstanding member. We are not told that she preached with her lips ; her hands were more eloquent. She listened to the great expositions given by the leaders of the assembly, and then methodically practised her doctrines. Probably she won much sympathy for the new cause, and the great preachers of her time had increased audiences because of the influence of this delightful woman.

The Woman Who Praised the Lord—Exodus 15:20, 21

" And Miriam the prophetess, the sister of Aaron, took a timbrel in her hand ; and all the women went out after her with timbrels and with dances. And Miriam answered them, Sing ye to the Lord, for he hath triumphed gloriously ; the horse and his rider hath he thrown into the sea." That ancient morning was destined to find an imperishable place in history. Israel had been redeemed from bondage ; mercy had triumphed over judgment, and the hearts of the women thrilled with the songs of deliverance. Language was inadequate to express the escaping emotions of these rejoicing hearts, and with glorious abandon they danced for joy.

Thus in all ages women have played their part. Some quietly pray while others, specially gifted by God, seek to tell the story of Christ. Some wistfully listen to the preachers, and then with constancy of purpose practise the principles of the faith. It's a far cry from Miriam at the Red Sea to the Salvation Army girl in a city slum ; but God is changeless in all ages. He did, He still does, and He always will, find pleasure in the woman whose affection and talents are placed at His feet.

PAUL . . . and his advice about walking
(EPHESIANS 4-6)

Many Bible students regard the epistle to the Ephesians as the most profound of the Pauline letters. The apostle had been a pastor in this famous city of Asia, and during his ministry had introduced his people to the vital doctrines of Christianity. It was to be expected, therefore, that his letter would continue this tuition. Chapters 1-3 embody the revelation of Christian doctrine. The key-word is *know*. Chapters 4-6 present Christian responsibility. The key-word is *walk*. The purpose of this brief study is to reveal Paul's ideas concerning the characteristics of the Christian walk. It is commonly believed that policemen are known by their feet! It is an absolute certainty that Christians are known by theirs.

Christians Should Walk Worthily

"I therefore, the prisoner of the Lord, beseech you that ye walk worthy of the vocation wherewith ye are called" (Ephes. 4:1). This is the first requirement of all who profess faith in Christ. The Gospel of Christ supersedes all other teaching, and presents the incomparable beauties of grace. Outcasts become the children of God, and hope is brought within reach of every human being. The Gospel brings a new dignity to men and women; and fully conscious of this high and holy calling, every Christian should adorn the doctrines preached. His walk must be worthy of his Master.

Christians Should Walk Differently

"This I say therefore, and testify in the Lord, that ye henceforth walk not as other Gentiles walk . . ." (4:17). Conversion means the renunciation of former ideologies. Man becomes a follower of Christ, because he has reached the place where he believes that Christ alone leads to reality. If a man were completely satisfied with his former way of living, he would not become a Christian. His regeneration brings him into a new society of friends, where the new ideas are commonly shared. When a man continues to walk in paths which he has already denounced, either his confession of faith was hypocritical, or he has slipped again into the ways of sin.

Christians Should Walk Affectionately

"Be ye therefore followers of God, as dear children; And walk in love, as Christ also hath loved us . . ." (5:1, 2). As

Christ loved, so we must love. This rare plant cannot thrive where bitterness, fault-finding, and carnal criticism sour the soil. When discord ruins the Church, when enmity separates brethren, the entire purpose of the Lord is frustrated. John once asked a very important question. "He that loveth not his brother whom he hath seen, how can he love God whom he hath not seen?" (1 John 4:20).

Christians Should Walk Intelligently

"For ye were sometimes darkness, but now are ye light in the Lord: walk as children of light" (Ephes. 5:8). It is very disconcerting to see an athlete floundering in a bog. Avoiding obvious difficulties, the runner strains every nerve in the supreme effort to reach the winning post. It is wiser to lose a minute avoiding trouble than it is to waste an hour overcoming it. Light means illumination, and illumination means guidance. Finality, purpose, decision, are characteristics of the Christian pilgrimage. Tramps may wander indecisively, but Christians walk!

Christians Should Walk Circumspectly

"See then that ye walk circumspectly, not as fools, but as wise" (5:15). A deliberate walk is not, of necessity, a hurried walk. The Christian pilgrimage is a matter of direction, not speed! Sometimes it pays to make haste slowly! Imagine a cat hurrying over the broken glass on the top of a garden wall! Recognizing the dangers abounding in all directions, the wise animal slowly puts a foot here, another there, and proceeds with extreme care. Christians should learn this lesson.

Christians Should Walk Courageously

"Put on the whole armour of God ... having on the breastplate of righteousness; And your feet shod with the preparation of the gospel of peace; Above all taking the shield of faith ... the helmet of salvation ... the sword of the Spirit ..." (6:11-17). Success in Christian warfare largely depends upon stability in the Christian walk. Great knowledge of the doctrines of Christ is negatived unless those identical truths are demonstrated in daily experience. Some people stand on their heads, but God made us to stand on our feet. The Christian walk is the foundation of all spiritual realities.

PAUL . . . who wrote the shortest life-story of Christ

(PHILIPPIANS 2: 5-13)

Paul was an expert at expressing much in little. His epistles encompassed eternal doctrines; his vision spanned untold periods of time; and through the medium of one sentence, the Christian philosopher expressed the heart of God. He was expert in the art of conciseness, but the Epistle to the Philippians presents his greatest masterpiece. Within the short space of six verses he wrote the life-story of the Son of God. Theologians of all ages have expanded and enlarged that original effort; the libraries of a world are filled with books illustrating the essay; the teachers of all Churches preach series of exhausting sermons about these striking texts. Yet long ago Paul sat quietly on his bench in a Roman prison, and with an ease so characteristic of the man, he expressed the inexpressible in 118 words. It was the shortest and greatest biography ever written.

A Glorious Christ

"Who, being in the form of God, thought it not robbery to be equal with God." One translation of the original text supplies food for thought. "Deity was not a thing to be grasped at." Since He already possessed it, there was no need to covet it. He was in the form of God, and to possess and claim the attributes of the Godhead was not an unlawful exercise. These were His by right. "And of the angels he saith, Who maketh his angels spirits, and his ministers a flame of fire. But *unto the Son* he saith, *Thy throne, O God,* is for ever and ever" (Heb. 1:7, 8). Thus, even as He claimed, He was there in the beginning with God. In His immortal prayer Jesus said, "And now, O Father, glorify thou me with thine own self, with the glory which I had with thee before the world was" (John 17:5). Paul sat on his bench and clearly saw the unrivalled splendour of those ancient times.

A Grievous Cross

"But made himself of no reputation, and took upon him the form of a servant, and was made in the likeness of men: And being found in fashion as a man, he humbled himself, and became obedient unto death, even the death of the cross." Perhaps at this juncture Paul paused and remembered his other brilliant effort at conciseness—"For ye know the grace of our Lord Jesus Christ, that, though he was rich, yet for your sakes he became poor, that ye through his poverty might become rich" (2 Cor. 8:9). Christ went to our cross that we might go to His heaven. He introduced eternal wealth into human poverty, that our unlimited limitations might be obliterated by His sufficiency. "... even the death of the cross." Immeasurable need challenged immortal love; and in the ensuing conflict, love triumphed.

A Glad Coronation

"Wherefore God also hath highly exalted him, and given him a name which is above every name: That at the name of Jesus every knee should bow...." The homegoing of the Saviour beggared description. All heaven awaited His coming, and when God said, "Sit on my right hand until I make thine enemies thy footstool," all the sons of God sang together for joy. The eternal Son was home again! Once in the end of the age He had appeared to put away sin by the sacrifice of Himself. Acclaimed by highest heaven, He sat at the right hand of the Majesty on high, where God crowned Him with glory and honour.

A Great Confession

Paul paused, and allowed his thoughts to race ahead through the years. This is the prerogative of all seers. Time and distance are meaningless to all who have looked into the face of God. Paul saw the end, the ultimate triumph; and once again his pen moved on the parchment. "And that every tongue should confess that Jesus Christ is Lord, to the glory of God the Father." Paul and John were brothers indeed, for when the beloved disciple similarly witnessed the final triumph, he said, "And he hath on his vesture and on his thigh a name written, KING OF KINGS, AND LORD OF LORDS" (Rev. 19:16). Evil may win occasional battles, but the ultimate triumph rests with God.

A Gracious Command

We must remember that this short life-story was written so that we could emulate Christ's example. "Let this mind be in you, which was also in Christ Jesus...." And when Paul had finished his biographical sketch, he urged the Philippians to work out their own salvation with fear and trembling. What God in grace has wrought in our hearts, we must work out in daily practice. The path to the cross leads also to the throne; but if we would reach the goal we must never turn back.

THE PRECIOUS BLOOD OF CHRIST ...
the master-key
(COLOSSIANS 1: 20)

Every New Testament preacher, and all New Testament writings, make reference to *the blood of Christ*. The theme is a scarlet thread running through the entire length of evangelical theology. Early in the sacred writings God revealed that the life was in the blood (Gen. 9:4), and in the New Testament the blood of Christ is synonymous with the life of Christ. Consequently the shed blood of Christ refers to His sinless life outpoured at Calvary. Whatever liberal theology might maintain, one fact is indisputable: that the apostles and leaders of the New Testament Church believed that man's salvation was procured through the sacrifice of Christ.

The Blood of Christ Made Peace for Sinners

"And, having made peace through the blood of his cross, by him to reconcile all things unto himself ..." (Col. 1:20). Man was at war with God; a state of open rebellion existed in the human soul. When divine justice demanded retribution, the Lord Jesus voluntarily identified Himself with the guilty people, and accepted the full responsibility of their sins. He carried their guilt to Calvary, and thereby secured an armistice. Thus the righteousness of God was vindicated, and a way was opened whereby the state of war might be terminated.

The Blood of Christ Brings People into a New Fellowship

"That at that time ye were without Christ, being aliens from the commonwealth of Israel, and strangers from the covenants of promise, having no hope, and without God in the world: But now in Christ Jesus ye who sometimes were far off are made nigh by the blood of Christ" (Ephes. 2:12, 13). Through the reconciling work of Christ, a new harmony was created. Man-made barriers and racial discrimination were superseded by the Christian Church. Masters and slaves sat together at the Lord's table as brethren. The peace secured at the cross became experimental in the souls of men, when the message of redemption reached out to the far country to bring aliens into the serenity of a new fellowship.

The Blood of Christ Cleanseth From Sin

"But if we walk in the light, as he is in the light, we have fellowship one with another, and the blood of Jesus Christ his Son cleanseth us from all sin " (1 John 1:7). Entrance into the fellowship of the Church does not guarantee immunity from sin. The Christian life means conflict and ceaseless watchfulness against the powers of evil. John stresses the fact that the death of Christ meets the needs of people for all time. " The precious blood of Christ *goes on* cleansing us from sin."

The Blood of Christ Enables Man to Enter the Presence of God

" Having therefore, brethren, boldness to enter into the holiest by the blood of Jesus, by a new and living way, which he hath consecrated for us . . ." (Heb. 10:19, 20). The epistle to the Hebrews provides striking contrasts between the old and new covenants. Formerly one man, the high priest, drew near to God on the day of atonement. Other people were excluded from the place of communion. The Saviour introduced a " better covenant," for through His death all men may enter into the presence of God, and find grace to help in time of need. Here is a progression of thought. Every man brought from the far country to enjoy the fellowship of saints, is not only assured of perpetual cleansing; he is provided with the master-key which unlocks every problem.

The Blood of Christ Overcomes Satan

" And I heard a loud voice saying in heaven . . . the accuser of our brethren is cast down. . . . And they overcame him by the blood of the Lamb, and by the word of their testimony; and they loved not their lives unto the death. Therefore rejoice ye heavens . . ." (Rev. 12:10-12). Here is a great mystery; here is glorious truth. *The power of the precious blood of Christ* is the greatest weapon ever used in holy warfare. Defeat is impossible when the hand of prayer wields it correctly.

The Blood of Christ Provides the Theme of Eternal Songs

" And they sung a new song, saying . . . Thou hast redeemed us to God by thy blood . . . and the number of them was ten thousand times ten thousand and thousands of thousands . . ." (Rev. 5:9-12). Probably many of the memories of earth will disappear amid eternal splendour; but the Cross will never be forgotten.

> Precious, precious blood of Jesus,
>   Shed on Calvary;
> Shed for rebels, shed for sinners,
>   Shed for me.

PAUL ... who believed in the return of his Lord
(1 THESSALONIANS 1–5)

It has been suggested that Paul wrote the second Epistle to the Thessalonians in order to correct mistakes made in his first Epistle. Some theologians suggest that Paul was deceived into thinking that the return of Christ was imminent; that eventually he recognized the absurdity of this belief, and endeavoured to correct the false impression made by his earlier writings. It is very difficult to accept this suggestion, for Paul repeats in his second epistle the statements already made. Although he does not again deal at length with the doctrines of the return of Christ, we are justified in assuming that since the Thessalonians were already acquainted with the Pauline message, there was no need to repeat what they already knew. Paul's first letter to the saints at Thessalonia included five short chapters, and it is significant that each one closed with a reference to the great Hope.

Conversion and His Coming

"... ye turned to God from idols to serve the living and true God; And to wait for his Son from heaven, whom he raised from the dead, even Jesus, which delivered us from the wrath to come" (1:9, 10). Perhaps this was the most fitting way in which the apostle could begin his letter. The new message revealed the folly of idolatry, and outlined the matchless wonder of the grace of God in Christ. Paul said, "And ye became followers of us, and of the Lord, having received the word in much affliction, with joy of the Holy Ghost: So that ye were ensamples to all that believe in Macedonia and Achaia." The promise of the coming of Christ was a most important part of the Gospel message. This was the positive affirmation made by every New Testament preacher, and every convert intelligently expected Christ's return. Modern preaching seems to fall short of the ancient standard.

Continuance and His Coming

"... for ye also have suffered like things of your own countrymen, even as they have of the Jews: Who both killed the Lord Jesus, and their own prophets, and have persecuted us ... but we brethren ... endeavoured the more abundantly to see your face with great desire.... For what is our hope, or joy, or crown of rejoicing? Are not even ye in the presence of our Lord Jesus Christ at his coming?" (2:14-19). Paul did not hesitate to express his deep appreciation of the faithful continuance of his converts. Persecution had not daunted them, for with steadfastness of purpose they were determined to remain loyal. The fact that Christ would return provided that extra incentive to be true in spite of persecution. The great Hope provided constant strength.

Consecration and His Coming

"And the Lord make you to increase and abound in love one toward another, and toward all men, even as we do toward you. To the end he may establish your hearts unblameable in holiness before God, even our Father, at the coming of our Lord Jesus Christ with all his saints" (3:12, 13). Paul agreed with John who said, "And every man that hath this hope in him purifieth himself, even as he is pure" (1 John 3:3). The teaching concerning the return of Christ was the heart of the New Testament message, and demanded the purity of the people who proclaimed it. The continuous expectation of Christ's return deepened personal desires for holiness.

Comfort and His Coming

"But I would not have you to be ignorant, brethren, concerning them which are asleep, that ye sorrow not, even as others which have no hope. For if we believe that Jesus died and rose again, even so them also which sleep in Jesus will God bring with him. . . . For the Lord himself shall descend from heaven . . . and the dead in Christ shall rise first: Then we which are alive and remain shall be caught up together with them in the clouds, to meet the Lord in the air: and so shall we ever be with the Lord. Wherefore *comfort one another* with these words" (4:13-18). The return of Christ would mean glad reunion with loved ones who had already fallen asleep. This message produced unending comfort in the hearts of the saints. Finally, Paul ended his letter with another reference to the great expectation, "And the very God of peace sanctify you wholly . . . unto the coming of our Lord Jesus Christ" (5:23). The return of the Saviour was the thrilling hope of the Church—it still is, for all who are not ashamed to meet Him.

ONESIPHORUS ... who loved to visit a prison
(2 Timothy 1: 16-18)

Some of the lesser known New Testament characters were among the best of God's servants. Their greatness was revealed not in eloquent preaching, but in courageous loyalty to Christ in the hour of peril. It is easier to be a faithful Christian when one is surrounded by friends and not by strangers. The very fact that one is being watched gives strength in the time of temptation. Yet, when one is true to Christ in a strange city, where it would be easy to compromise, that is the test of loyalty. Onesiphorus was a man of this calibre. We are not told the nature of the business which took him to Rome, but it is to his eternal credit that during his stay there he determined to visit the imprisoned Paul.

How Great His Courage

The apostle wrote to Timothy, " The Lord give mercy unto the house of Onesiphorus; for he oft refreshed me, and was not ashamed of my chain: But, when he was in Rome, he sought me out very diligently, and found me." The Romans did not consider Paul to be a glamorous hero. He was a preacher of an alien faith, an enemy of the empire, and a danger to the community. Ultimately he would be executed. Even his associates were suspect, and perhaps it was for this reason that Paul admitted, " Only Luke is with me." Yet this visitor to the imperial city persistently made his enquiries until he was able to locate his friend. He overcame every difficulty, and at the risk of his own liberty succeeded in reaching and ministering to Paul. Was he a convert of the great apostle? Did he owe his spiritual experiences to the inspired ministry of the fearless leader? We are not told. Yet it is clear that resolute courage was an outstanding characteristic of this obscure saint, who but for this visit to Rome might never have been mentioned in the sacred record.

How Great His Constancy

Paul continued, " The Lord grant unto him that he may obtain mercy of the Lord in that day: and in how many things he ministered unto me at Ephesus, thou knowest very well." This was not the first time Paul had been indebted to this gracious believer. At some time during the apostle's ministry in Asia, Onesiphorus had been invaluable to the pioneer missionary. We cannot be sure what length of time had elapsed between the two occasions, but it is most refreshing to remember that the passing of time had not changed this

Christian. Unlike many of the Galatians, whose early successes were offset by later indifference, this man had apparently mastered the secret of "running with patience the race that was set before him." At home in Ephesus, and away in Rome, in fair weather and in foul, Onesiphorus demonstrated the reality of his faith in Christ. Paul was certainly cheered to see the familiar face, and his words, "he oft refreshed me, and was not ashamed of my chain," seem to suggest that the prisoner had many visits from the man of Ephesus.

How Great His Confession

It is said that "actions speak louder than words," and this is very evident in the story of Onesiphorus. We are not told that he ever preached to crowds of people. Probably he was not a great orator. Yet the magnificent influence of his confession may be judged by the fact that Paul could speak of "the household of Onesiphorus" (2 Tim. 4:19). The continued consecration of this man had influenced his family in favour of Christ. One of the enigmas of life is that oftentimes Christian parents have unbelieving children. Happy indeed is the father whose influence for Christ completely charms and attracts his family into the kingdom of God. It would appear that the family of Onesiphorus had watched and listened as he practised the faith he believed, and the reality of his unending consecration made it easy for them to follow his glorious example. They were known to Paul, and it was with great sincerity that the imprisoned apostle prayed, "The Lord give mercy to the house of Onesiphorus." And as suddenly as he appeared on the pages of the New Testament, so this gracious character disappeared again. Perhaps he was not a great leader of a Church; maybe he never attained to the office of a deacon; yet his courageous, dependable devotion won for him a place among the immortals.

PAUL . . . who met a prodigal son
(Epistle to Philemon)

What a pity it is that there is no telephone exchange in heaven! Of course, there is a private line to the palace of the King, and all praying people use it. But what a shame the service is not extended! If only we could lift a receiver, dial a number, and ask the angelic operator to put us through to Paul the apostle. If only this were possible, the industries of the world would be still while all men listened. The people in palaces and hovels would desire to hear the message, and during that conversation all other voices would be hushed. Wishful thinking! Certainly, and perhaps a little absurd; but it does no harm. It merely represents the fact that if it were possible, Paul would be able to supply the answers to many of our questions. For example, we could ask him about his convert Onesimus.

Grace Redeeming

The Acts of the Apostles closes with the words: "And Paul dwelt two whole years in his own hired house, and received all that came unto him, Preaching the kingdom of God, and teaching those things which concern the Lord Jesus Christ, with all confidence, no man forbidding him." Probably this was the first Christian pastorate in Rome; and Paul's Church was established in a simple home. Were all the meetings held in the house, or was Paul permitted to walk to the market place? Did he ever minister in the synagogue, and where did he find Onesimus—or did Onesimus find him? Had the fugitive become destitute in a strange city, and did desperation drive him to Paul? Had he become contrite, and did he miserably seek advice from the only man he knew in the city? Was Onesimus surprised when he recognized the preacher? Oh, Paul, why can't we get you on the 'phone? Surely, you were thrilled to lead that man to Christ.

Grace Repaying

Paul wrote, "I beseech thee for my son Onesimus, whom I have begotten in my bonds. Which in time past was to thee unprofitable, but now profitable both to thee and to me. . . . Whom I would have retained with me, that in thy stead he might have ministered unto me in the bonds of the gospel." It is therefore clear that grace had completely transformed Onesimus. He had no wish to escape from Paul; and in contrast to Demas and others, this new convert loved to serve the man who had won him for Christ. Grace had been shed abroad in his heart. His presence cheered Paul, and his eagerness both to learn and to help demonstrated the reality of his conversion. The transparent sincerity of this babe in Christ, and the whole-hearted service which he rendered, might well serve as an example for all saints.

Grace Restoring

Paul was a little sad, and Onesimus had downcast eyes. The apostle was speaking: " Son, I must send you home, and I don't want to do it. I could wish that you were here for ever. But Philemon is your master, and the fact that God has forgiven your sin does not free you from the obligation to make restitution for the wrongs of the past. Moral requirements demand that you return to the man to whom you are indebted. My boy, you must go home." And Onesimus agreed. Amazing changes had taken place since he had absconded from his master. Punishment might be waiting for him, but he found comfort in the fact that he was about to do his duty. He had written a letter at Paul's dictation, and that letter—the epistle to Philemon—was a document destined to become famous throughout the world.

Grace Replying

Philemon's eyes were misty; the letter from his old friend had stirred memory. Again and again he read, " I beseech thee for my son Onesimus, whom I have begotten in my bonds. . . . He departed from thee for a season, that thou shouldest receive him for ever; Not now as a servant, but above a servant, a brother beloved, specially to me, but now much more unto thee, *both in the flesh,* and in the Lord." The words " both in the flesh " suggest that Onesimus might have been a brother of Philemon—a prodigal brother who had stolen money. One does not need great imagination to see a cosy parlour where a log fire burns on the hearth. The elder brother listens to this story of a conversion in Rome. Former wrongs were all forgotten; bitterness of spirit was completely unknown, and love reigned amid boundless rejoicing. Yes, this is a story of grace—wonderful grace overflowing in four hearts.

CHRIST . . . and the nastiest taste in the world
(HEBREWS 2: 9)

The term *death* has a threefold interpretation in the Scriptures. (i) Death is the termination of life's earthly journey. It is the experience which, through sickness, accident, or age, eventually overcomes man, and removes him from conscious association with fellow beings. (ii) Death is used to express the state of unregenerate men. They are said to be dead in trespasses and sins; and by that term is inferred the fact that they are unresponsive to the promptings of the Spirit of God. (iii) Death is the ultimate tragedy which overwhelms the guilty. When a sinful world appears before the throne of God, each man will be judged according to the facts written in God's records. "And they were judged every man according to their works. And death and hell were cast into the lake of fire. This is the second death" (Rev. 20:13, 14). There are certain texts of holy Scripture which can only be understood as they are examined in the light of these facts.

Death and the Critics

And the Lord Jesus said, "Verily I say unto you, There be some standing here, which shall not taste of death, till they see the Son of man coming in his kingdom" (Matt. 16:28). This was an outstanding utterance, and can only mean one thing. It will be immediately recognized that neither of the first two interpretations could possibly explain the text. The people to whom Christ referred were hypocrites, and were said to be "whited sepulchres"; bigoted zealots who were expert at finding faults in all hearts but their own. They were already dead in sin. We do not know how long they survived, but it is perfectly safe to say they were buried long ago; while the promise of Christ's coming still awaits fulfilment. It follows that the only possible interpretation of the text is one which takes our thoughts into the future. Christ realized the undying hatred of His enemies, and boldly pronounced that before final doom overtook His critics, they would witness His triumph. And in that one statement He reaffirmed His belief in the survival of the soul. He recognized that physical death was not annihilation, but an introduction to a new world. He also declared His belief in the final judgment. "They shall not taste of death *till* they see the Son of man coming in his kingdom."

Death and the Christ

"But we see Jesus, who was made a little lower than the angels for the suffering of death, crowned with glory and honour; that he by the grace of God *should taste death for every man*" (Heb. 2:9). The Lord Jesus was never dead in sins, for "he was in all points tempted like as we are, yet without sin" (4:15). And it is also extremely difficult to understand how His succumbing to physical weakness could materially affect every man. Unless there be spiritual truth connected with His sacrifice, then a death 2,000 years ago could hardly affect modern people. The second death means separation from God; a state of inexpressible remorse; the outcome of lost opportunities; the inevitable reward of sin. "Christ tasted death for every man." He took our sins, and went into the darkness. When the three hours of impenetrable blackness gave place to the new dawn, Christ uttered a cry of glad relief. He said, "My God, my God, why *didst* thou forsake me?" The aorist tense of the verb is used in this connection, revealing something completely accomplished in the past. The work was finished; the struggle had ended. Christ had been in the dark so that we could remain in the light for ever.

Death and the Christian

"Then said the Jews unto him, Now we know that thou hast a devil. Abraham is dead, and the prophets; and thou sayest, If a man keep my saying, *he shall never taste of death*" (John 8:52). It is not difficult to appreciate the problems of those Jewish hearers. It seemed fantastic that this Carpenter should speak such apparent absurdities. Yet as Paul afterward declared, "These things are spiritually discerned." Jesus said unto Martha, "I am the resurrection, and the life: he that believeth in me, though he were dead, yet shall he live: And whosoever liveth and believeth in me, shall never die" (John 11:25, 26). Once again two interpretations are instantly ruled out. Since we were born in sin and shapen in iniquity, and since countless thousands of saints have passed through the valley of the shadow of death, the text can only mean one thing. The Christian will never know the anguish of eternal condemnation, because in Christ he has been pardoned. The Lord Jesus said, "They shall not come into condemnation" (John 5:24). We shall never taste the bitterness of eternal death, because He tasted it for us.

THE ROYAL HIGHWAY ... or milestones on the road to heaven

(EPISTLE TO THE HEBREWS)

The epistle to the Hebrews was written to help people whose faith had been rudely shaken. Why should saints be fed to hungry lions if their new faith pleased God? If the new High Priest had superseded the old, why did He not intercede more effectively, and so prevent the catastrophes which were overwhelming the Church? The epistle to the Hebrews answered these questions, and set forth clearly the benefits of the " better covenant." Its appeals were concise and thought-provoking, and when viewed together they provide a comprehensive view of the requirements of the Christian faith.

"*Let us labour therefore to enter into that rest*"—Hebrews 4:11

" There remaineth therefore a rest for the people of God," and every saint should persistently strive toward the desired goal. The path may be difficult ; but with tenacity of purpose, men must strive to reach the ultimate haven. Israel had failed in their quest, and their dismal effort should serve as a warning to the Church. When the glorious land of Canaan lay before them, they had permitted unbelief to blind their eyes, and consequently had perished in the wilderness.

"*Let us hold fast our profession*"—Hebrews 4:14

" Seeing then that we have a great high priest ... let us hold fast our profession. For we have not a high priest who cannot be touched with the feeling of our infirmities ; but was in all points tempted like as we are, yet without sin." The knowledge that the Lord has walked our pathway should stimulate faith ; and determined to hold what we possess, we should cling tenaciously to the teachings already received. Thus we prepare the way for further advances.

"*Let us therefore come boldly unto the throne of grace*"—Hebrews 4:16

In this way we shall obtain mercy, and find grace to help us in time of need. Communion with God is indispensable if we are to advance along the royal highway. Prevailing prayer quietens the soul and secures the grace which alone can offset the dangers and difficulties of the path. A pilgrim who does not pray will become a tramp. A pilgrim journeys ; a tramp meanders!

" Let us go on unto perfection "—Hebrews 6:1

". . . not laying again the foundation of repentance from dead works, and of faith toward God." Thus in one lucid statement the writer of this epistle provides a soul-thrilling glimpse of the upward way. John declares: " When he shall appear we shall be like him." Regeneration is but the introduction to the inexhaustible riches of Christ. Much, much more awaits the man who walks with God.

" Let us consider one another "—Hebrews 10:24

Fellowship with the saints is indispensable for the nurture of the soul, and to abstain from meeting with other travellers is both unwise and contrary to the will of God. They who would be helped must themselves render help; that love might characterize the assembly, and that every root of bitterness might be removed from the hearts of all who profess allegiance to Christ.

" Let us have grace "—Hebrews 12:28

"Wherefore we receiving a kingdom which cannot be moved, let us have grace, whereby we may serve God acceptably with reverence and godly fear." When the love of God is shed abroad in our hearts, therefore follows an outflow of reverence toward the Lord, and an overflow of grace toward fellow men. Only thus can we serve God satisfactorily; only thus can we adorn the faith we preach.

" Let us go forth therefore unto him . . . bearing his reproach "
—Hebrews 13:13

Sometimes the path of Christian service runs through enemy territory. We must expect to encounter great difficulties, and be prepared to withstand fierce persecution. The Master was often despised and rejected, and it is to be expected that sometimes the same fate may overtake His followers. Should this happen, we must choose " rather to suffer affliction with the people of God, than to enjoy the pleasures of sin for a season."

" Let us offer the sacrifice of praise to God continually "—
Hebrews 13:15

". . . that is, the fruit of our lips giving thanks to his name." If we walk the appointed pathway, joy will overflow in our hearts. Then we shall be able to enter into His presence with thanksgiving, and into His courts with praise. This is the royal highway; and happy indeed is that man whose feet never stray from its course.

GOD'S ART GALLERY ... and three of its wonderful pictures
(Hebrews 11 : 29-31)

The writer of this epistle has created an art gallery in which the greatest spiritual portraits are on display. The artist used a brush called faith, and while some of these pictures are alone in splendid magnificence, here and there some are grouped together—they are displayed in series. For example, the pictures of Israel, Jericho, and Rahab, suggest an inspiring progression of New Testament teaching.

The Divided Waters (v. 29)

This portrait is a masterpiece! The scene depicted is one where hope struggles to overcome abject despair. Israel, so recently delivered from Egyptian bondage, looks back at the pursuing enemy. Hemmed in by hills, and halted by the sea, it could only be a matter of time before Pharaoh again subjugated the fearful people. The women clutch their children, and are terrified; the helpless men bite their lips in vexation. In the forefront of the scene, the artist has placed Moses with rod lifted high. See, the waters are going back. It is unbelievable!—God has opened a highway through the sea. Moses smiles and waves his people on; but just for a moment they hesitate, as three awful possibilities loom before them. (i) Would they sink in the mire left by receding waters? (ii) Would the waters return to overwhelm them? (iii) Would the dangers of the new land be too great? These suggestions find a response in many hearts; for all three are apt to recur when a man faces the challenge of the unknown. When he obeys the command of God, will he be overcome by weakness? Will spiritual emotions be swamped by the crashing waters of temptation? Will the conflicts of the new life be too fierce?

The Destroyed Walls (v. 30)

The artist's second effort is no less picturesque. The nomadic peoples of the Jericho plains have retired into their fortress city. The gates are closed, and the watchmen are on the walls. The invaders move toward the citadel. Jericho is the first of the Canaanite cities to be taken, and the task seems to be hopeless. How can inexperienced people conquer without arms? How can indescribable weakness overcome planned strength? It cannot be done! But Joshua smiles. He has been in touch with God, and knows exactly what to do. The long procession encircles the city; and but for the fear which grips their hearts, even the Canaanites would laugh. It is ludicrous. These people were substituting the blast of bugles for battering rams! Around and around they go, and the whole scene savours of fantasy. And then the earth trembles; the walls bulge outwards, and the last line of defence is flattened. These strange people of God possess a secret weapon against which no army can stand. By faith they crossed the sea; by faith they conquer Jericho. Saving faith brought them from bondage; the same faith enables them to walk with God. This is the second lesson in Christian experience.

The Delivered Woman (v. 31)

We stand before the third picture of this inspiring group, and the scene is animated! The fallen masonry of Jericho's ruined walls can be seen everywhere. Smoke furiously billows from burning homes, while relentless soldiers probe the narrow alley-ways. Yet in the forefront of the scene a woman stands with her back to an undamaged part of the wall, upon which stands her home. Clearly, a scarlet thread hangs from her window frame. We remember the commands given by Israel's men. Probably the idea had been suggested by the fact that long before their people had acted similarly in Egypt. The blood on the doorposts and lintels of their homes had been a preventative of judgment. Hence Rahab the harlot was instructed to act similarly, and her obedience saved her life. Yes, this is a very thought-provoking trio of Old Testament portraits. The first suggests freedom from the bondage of sin—Egypt was left behind. The second suggests freedom from the dominion of sin—Jericho was taken. The third might easily suggest freedom from the presence of sin—Rahab the harlot escaped judgment and became a dignified woman of God. These were mere shadows of reality; but they clearly illustrate the central message of the Gospel. *By faith they passed through.* Faith is the key to every problem; and no man need be bankrupt when heaven's treasure house is before him!

JOHN . . . and his yardstick of truth
(THIRD EPISTLE OF JOHN)

The apostle John was worried. Frowns of perplexity were appearing upon his face, for the most sacred things in life were being denied. Apostles and Church leaders had been taken to their eternal home, and he alone remained of the original party. Heresy was spreading in all directions, and many people denied that Christ had come in the flesh. Their eloquence equalled their arrogance, and the doctrinal standards of the Church were being ruthlessly destroyed. John had already written two epistles in which he condemned the new teaching; but now as he sat with his pen in his hand, he had certain things to say concerning some of his fellow believers and their relationship to *truth*. Either his message was false or it had been sent by God, and in the light of that standard all teaching had to be examined.

A Great Fellowship

"The elder unto the well beloved Gaius, *whom I love in the truth*" (3 John 1). Not the least among the wonders of grace was the fact that redeeming love united men of all types into a fellowship which surpassed anything else in the world. Barbarian, Scythian; bond and free; Jew, Greek, and Roman, took their respective places in the living edifice known as the Church of Christ. These people loved each other, for racial enmity, social dissension, and other man-made divisions ceased to exist within the boundaries of the Christian fellowship. These people called each other brethren, and when circumstances demanded, the wealthy sacrificed their possessions in order to increase the common fund from which less fortunate brethren received assistance. John had written earlier, "But whoso hath this world's good, and seeth his brother have need, and shutteth up his bowels of compassion from him, how dwelleth the love of God in him? My little children, let us not love in word, neither in tongue; but in deed and in truth" (1 John 3:17, 18).

A Great Follower

"For I rejoiced greatly, when the brethren came and testified of the truth that is in thee, *even as thou walkest in truth*. I have no greater joy than to hear that my children walk in truth" (vv. 3, 4). We cannot fail to see how John couples internal convictions with the external walk. Fellowship in the secret place provides the inspiration for a public profession of faith. Gaius reiterated the word of the Psalmist, "Thy word have I hid in my heart, that I might not sin against thee." The truth reigned supreme within his Christian kingdom. And every word and deed issuing from his regal heart evoked divine favour. He walked calmly with his Lord, and every detail of his conduct harmonized with God's will.

A Great Fellow-Helper

"Beloved, thou doest faithfully whatsoever thou doest to the brethren, and to strangers; Which have borne witness of thy charity before the church: whom if thou bring forward on their journey after a godly sort, thou shalt do well. Because that for his name's sake they went forth, taking nothing of the Gentiles. We therefore ought to receive such, *that we might be fellow helpers to the truth*" (vv. 5-8). Once again *the truth* appears as John's yardstick. Every matter of life and service is measured against this infallible standard. Nothing matters but the revealed will and word of God. Within the ranks of the Christian Church was something far more wonderful than mere sentiment. Any man, believing the truth, and living to preach it, had the right to expect the utmost co-operation of his brethren. One man preached, and another entertained the preacher; but both played an important part in the work of Christ. Even in those early days Diotrephes had developed a standard of Church ruling which insisted on every man subscribing to his own personal likes and dislikes. John said, "He receiveth us not." Any man who refused to accept John at the Lord's Table was a self-made god who worshipped at his own shrine. Diotrephes was the progenitor of a sect which still remains.

A Great Fame

"Demetrius hath a good report of all men, *and of the truth itself . .*" (v. 12). To be commended of the truth represents the greatest reward in life. This is the Lord's saying, "Well done, thou good and faithful servant." John's statement supplies a thought-provoking couplet. When a man is commended of the truth, he is also commended of men. There is something radically wrong with an unattractive Christian!

THE CHURCH AT PERGAMOS ... and the little white stone

(REVELATION 2: 17)

Diamonds are sometimes discovered in a desolate wilderness; and in like manner, some of the greatest Bible treasures are found in unlikely places. There are certain Scriptures which instantly yield their gems; there are others where rare jewels still await discovery. This fact is clearly illustrated in Christ's letter to the Church at Pergamos. At the conclusion of His message, the Lord says, " To him that overcometh will I give to eat of the hidden manna, and will give him a white stone, and in the stone a new name written, which no man knoweth saving he that receiveth it." This verse provides one of the most delightful word-pictures found in the New Testament.

The Stone of Witness

Hotels and inns were almost non-existent in Bible lands, and oftentimes a traveller journeying into new territory had to search diligently in order to find accommodation. Homes were few and far between, yet no householder refused hospitality if circumstances enabled him to entertain visitors. A traveller was permitted to enter the home and to stay as long as his business required. Adequate payment would be made for this kindness, but in addition, and according to the custom of the land, before he departed the guest produced a small white stone already cleverly divided into two parts. He always retained the one half, but the other was given to the host. The departing visitor would explain that some day the host might have occasion to travel in other lands, and in the event of his reaching a certain locality, he should call at the given address. If he needed hospitality he would be wise to produce his half of the white stone. It should be a stone of witness between both men. Should the one-time host need accommodation, he whom he had previously welcomed, would be delighted to return the kindness.

The Stone of Welcome

The small stone would be gratefully accepted and stored in a safe place, and when the owner had occasion to visit his friend's district, he would present himself at the home of his former guest. If a number of years had elapsed, it might be that the householder had forgotten the face of his former benefactor; but any doubt concerning the matter was instantly dispelled when the caller produced the half section of the white stone. The host would examine it, and read the name written thereon, and with lights of recollection shining in his eyes he would open the door of his homestead and say, " Welcome. As you welcomed me to your heart and home when I journeyed in your land, so now it is my privilege to do likewise for you. Friend, come in." Within the warmth of the hospitable apartment, the two men would enjoy fellowship and recall the events of bygone days. The white stone of witness never failed to obtain admittance to the heart and home of the former traveller.

The Stone of Wealth

Thus, when Christ spoke to His Church, He urged them to overcome in the battles of life ; to resist evil and follow after righteousness ; and as a reward, He would give to them a white stone. When the great Traveller comes to sojourn in our country, we may welcome Him, and be sure that some day He will return the kindness. With the passing of the years, we shall leave our earthly abode and journey into those realms from which He came. The Lord Jesus promised that if we welcome Him here, He will welcome us there. And that is the doctrinal jewel hidden in the text, " To him that overcometh will I give . . . a white stone." The members of the Church at Pergamos, acquainted as they were with ancient customs, instantly recognized all the delightful facets of this scintillating Biblical diamond. They looked at it ; they admired it, and exultantly cried, " O grave, where is thy victory? O death, where is thy sting?" Death held no terrors for them, for it only registered the beginning of a journey when they went to meet an old Friend. To them, the Lord's white stone was the most precious jewel ever discovered. It represented eternal wealth. They would not have sold it for a king's ransom.

THE LAMB . . . the alpha and omega of God's revelation
(REVELATION 7: 14; 21: 27; 22: 17)

The Book of Revelation is like a great mountain range, the lower half of which is enshrouded in mists. The picturesque phraseology, the strange figures and forms, the attendant descriptions, are swirling cloud-banks obscuring our vision, and leaving us to guess what unrivalled beauties might lie in the shadows. Attracted rather than repelled by this barrier, many Bible students have plunged into the unknown. Their listeners have marvelled at the expository gems brought into the light; but some have become a little confused when other Christian mountaineers emerged with interpretations which seemed to contradict earlier findings. Fog can play peculiar tricks with vision, and all youthful Bible teachers might be well advised to explore less dangerous places. Nevertheless, the upper slopes of this great mountain range are plainly visible. They glisten and shine in the light of another world; their peaks point upward; and in spite of the underlying fog, they beckon the brave and the resourceful. Cut out in the rocks of these upper slopes, one imperishable name defies the ravages of time. That name is: *the Lamb*.

The Lamb's Blood Redeeming

This is a mountain peak of unrivalled beauty. The glades and glens of the lowlands lead to the sunlit pastures beyond. There the air is clear, and the flowers of Paradise nod in the breeze. Against the sombre background of Sinai, where the law thundered out to trembling man, this celestial eminence rises far above the fog and smoke of earth. It reaches to the throne of God, and provides a path by which all men can draw near to worship. It is truly a remarkable thing that sinners should ever find an entrance into the presence of God; yet it is far more wonderful that the Son of God should have become personally responsible for getting them there. He entered into the world to save sinners; and since the law stated that without the shedding of blood there could be no remission, He gladly laid down His life for men. Peter said, "You were not redeemed with corruptible things . . . but with the precious blood of Christ" (1 Peter 1: 18, 19). The saints in heaven reiterated these sentiments and sang a new song, "Thou art worthy . . . for thou hast redeemed us to God by thy blood" (Rev. 5:9). When John enquired concerning the people who were present before the throne of God, he was told, "These are they which . . . have washed their robes and made them white in the blood of the lamb" (7:14).

The Lamb's Book Revealing

"And I saw the dead, small and great, stand before God; and the books were opened: and another book was opened, which is the book of life: and the dead were judged out of those things which were written in the books, according to their works.... And whosoever was not found written in the book of life was cast into the lake of fire" (20:12-15). John wrote of the Holy City, "And there shall in no wise enter into it anything that defileth ... but they which are written in the lamb's book of life" (21:27). The text infers three vital things. (i) *God's records are true.* It may be taken for granted that the account will be accurate. What I am, He will record. (ii) *God's appointments are inescapable.* John stresses the fact that all men will stand before God. Their reluctance to do so will not provide a way of escape. This is an appointment no one can avoid. (iii) *God's decisions are final.* There is no court of appeal. Whatever is meant by the term "the lake of fire" is something each individual must consider personally. To say the least, any verdict leading to eternal rejection can be nothing short of tragic.

The Lamb's Bride Rejoicing

"And I saw a new heaven and a new earth: for the first heaven and the first earth were passed away.... And I John saw the holy city, new Jerusalem, coming down from God out of heaven, prepared as a bride adorned for her husband. And I heard a great voice out of heaven saying, Behold, the tabernacle of God is with men, and he will dwell with them, and they shall be his people, and God himself shall be with them.... And God shall wipe away all tears from their eyes; and there shall be no more death, neither sorrow nor crying, neither shall there be any more pain" (21:1-4). Finally, John recorded the words of his Lord, "I am the root and the offspring of David, and the bright and morning star. And the Spirit and the bride say, Come.... And let him that is athirst come. And whosoever will, let him take the water of life freely" (22:16, 17). Earth should be more than a playground. It should be the preparatory stage where wise people prepare for eternity. The Gospel of God says *come,* and no soul can be deaf when God is speaking.

ALPHABETICAL INDEX FOR BIBLE TREASURES

	PAGE
Abraham's Rogues	7
Abram's Exercises	5
Andrew	111
Apostles and Life Abundant	115
Apothecary, The	53
Barzillai	29
Christ and the Bread	107
Christ and the Bulldozer	81
Christ's Commentary	99
Christ's Invitation	71
Christ and the Nasty Taste	153
Christ's Prayer for Peter	105
Christ and Rare Fruit	119
Christ's Requirements	97
Christ's Silence	79
Christ's Tantalizing Inconsistency	121
Christ and Three Steps	109
Christ and Two Cities	85
Christ, The Unique	113
Christ and Values	87
Church at Pergamos, The	161
Church and Seventh Day, The	127
Church's Standard, The	55

	PAGE
Dagon	23
David's Giants	25
Elisha and the Children	35
Enoch and the Baby	3
Ezekiel's Sermon	65
Five Heads, The	89
Four Kings, The	21
Four Midgets, The	49
Funeral of John, The	77
Gardener, The	47
God's Art Gallery	157
Gold Digger, The	75
Good Shepherd, The	117
Great Wedding, The	83
Haggai's Punch	67
Holy Spirit and Sin	73
House of Mercy, The	103
Insignificance, Mr.	51
Isaiah Who Saw Love	59
Isaiah's Pen	61
Isaiah and Telescopic Sight	63
Isaiah's Wells	57
Jabez	37
Jehoiada and Joash	41
Jehoshaphat	39
Joab	31

	PAGE		PAGE
John's Yardstick	159	Paul and Onesimus	151
Joseph's Funeral	11	Paul and Second Advent	147
Joshua's Symbolism	19	Paul's Stubbornness	133
Lamb, The	163	Paul and Walking	141
Lawyer and Ruler, The	101	Paul and Women	139
Lot's Wife	9	Peter's Rebuke	125
		Peter's Greatest Shock	93
Man and Evolution	1	Precious Blood, The	145
Man and Withered Hand	95	Royal Highway, The	155
Moses and Christ	15		
Moses and the Eagle	17		
Moses and His Job	13	Saul Hypnotized	27
		Simon the Leper	91
Obadiah	33		
Onesiphorus	149	Two Men Who Triumphed	123
Paul and Barnabas	129		
Paul and Christ's Story	143	Uzziah	43
Paul and God's Salvation	137	Wise Birds, The	45
Paul's Ill Wind	135		
Paul's Mainspring	131	Zechariah's Picture	69

Combined and Comprehensive Bible Index Covering Bible Cameos—Bible Pinnacles—Bible Treasures

			PAGE
GENESIS:			
1:26	...	B. Treasures	114
2:8-9	...	B. Pinnacles	19
2:21-22	...	B. Pinnacles	1
3:10	...	B. Cameos	1
3:22	...	B. Cameos	131
3:22-24	...	B. Pinnacles	19
3:24	...	B. Pinnacles	6
4:1-10	...	B. Pinnacles	3
4:16-26	...	B. Treasures	1
5:21-22	...	B. Treasures	3
5:24	...	B. Pinnacles	5
6:20	...	B. Cameos	3
7:10	...	B. Pinnacles	167
9:4	...	B. Treasures	145
9:13	...	B. Pinnacles	168
13:1-4	...	B. Cameos	5
13:7-18	...	B. Treasures	5
18:9-15	...	B. Pinnacles	7
18:27	...	B. Treasures	7
19:16-22	...	B. Cameos	7
19:17	...	B. Treasures	9
19:26	...	B. Treasures	9
21:5	...	B. Pinnacles	9
21:14-19	...	B. Cameos	130
22:5	...	B. Pinnacles	9
22:8	...	B. Pinnacles	10
22:15-18	...	B. Pinnacles	10
24:1-10	...	B. Pinnacles	11
24:58-67	...	B. Pinnacles	11
25:21	...	B. Pinnacles	12
25:29-34	...	B. Cameos	11
26:18	...	B. Cameos	9
27:38	...	B. Cameos	12
28:2-11	...	B. Pinnacles	13
28:10-17	...	B. Pinnacles	13
32:24-35	...	B. Cameos	13
37:41	...	B. Cameos	15
50:25	...	B. Treasures	11
EXODUS:			
3:4	...	B. Treasures	13
3:13-14	...	B. Treasures	122

EXODUS: PAGE

12:2	B. Pinnacles	15
12:13	B. Pinnacles	167
13:17-19	B. Treasures	11
15:20-21	B. Treasures	140
15:22-23	B. Pinnacles	19
15:23-25	B. Pinnacles	19
31:10	B. Pinnacles	55
32:26	B. Pinnacles	17
40:1-17	B. Pinnacles	16

LEVITICUS:

20:6	B. Pinnacles	41
20:10	B. Cameos	137
20:27	B. Pinnacles	41

NUMBERS:

21:5-9	B. Treasures	15
21:8	B. Pinnacles	20
22:24	B. Cameos	17
35:30	B. Pinnacles	157

DEUTERONOMY:

18:10-12	B. Pinnacles	41
19:15	B. Pinnacles	157
28:1-15	B. Pinnacles	73
32:11	B. Treasures	17
34:5-6	B. Cameos	19

JOSHUA:

2:18-19	B. Pinnacles	21
2:18-19	B. Pinnacles	167
4:3-20	B. Treasures	19
5:13-15	B. Cameos	21
6:25	B. Pinnacles	21
7:1-6	B. Pinnacles	23
10:16	B. Treasures	21
13:12	B. Cameos	18
24:32	B. Treasures	12

JUDGES:

1:5-7	B. Pinnacles	25
1:12-13	B. Cameos	23
3:9-10	B. Cameos	24
6:30-31	B. Pinnacles	27
7:20	B. Pinnacles	27
11:7	B. Pinnacles	29
11:30-35	B. Pinnacles	29
16:17	B. Cameos	25
17:7-12	B. Pinnacles	31
18:11-31	B. Pinnacles	32
19:27-30	B. Pinnacles	33

			PAGE
JUDGES:			
20:1-2	...	B. Pinnacles	33
20:44-47	...	B. Pinnacles	33
RUTH:			
1:1-2	...	B. Cameos	27
1:19	...	B. Pinnacles	35
2:1	...	B. Pinnacles	22
4:17	...	B. Pinnacles	22
4:21-22	...	B. Pinnacles	36
1 SAMUEL:			
1:11-12	...	B. Treasures	139
1:11-13	...	B. Cameos	30
1:11-19	...	B. Pinnacles	164
2:12-17	...	B. Cameos	113
2:21	...	B. Cameos	29
5:4	...	B. Treasures	23
6:12	...	B. Treasures	24
11:1-3	...	B. Cameos	36
15:1-3	...	B. Pinnacles	37
15:23-28	...	B. Pinnacles	37
17:49	...	B. Treasures	25
19:19-24	...	B. Treasures	27
22:2	...	B. Pinnacles	40
22:14	...	B. Pinnacles	39
22:19-20	...	B. Pinnacles	39
22:21-23	...	B. Pinnacles	40
25	...	B. Cameos	31
28:6-7	...	B. Pinnacles	42
28:11-12	...	B. Pinnacles	41
30:11-18	...	B. Cameos	33
31:11-12	...	B. Cameos	35
2 SAMUEL:			
1:2-4	...	B. Pinnacles	45
2:20-23	...	B. Cameos	37
3:27	...	B. Cameos	37
6:11	...	B. Cameos	39
8:15-16	...	B. Treasures	31
11:3	...	B. Pinnacles	45
12:26-31	...	B. Treasures	32
13:39	...	B. Treasures	31
14:1-23	...	B. Pinnacles	43
15:12	...	B. Pinnacles	46
16:3-4	...	B. Cameos	44
16:5-8	...	B. Cameos	41
16:20-23	...	B. Pinnacles	46
17:23	...	B. Pinnacles	45
17:27-29	...	B. Treasures	29
19:15-23	...	B. Cameos	41

			PAGE
2 SAMUEL:			
19:24	...	B. Cameos	43
19:33-37	...	B. Treasures	29
20:15-19	...	B. Treasures	51
23:34	...	B. Pinnacles	45
24:10	...	B. Pinnacles	47
24:24	...	B. Pinnacles	47
1 KINGS:			
1:7	...	B. Treasures	31
1:8	...	B. Cameos	42
1:45-50	...	B. Cameos	45
2:1-9	...	B. Cameos	42
2:3-6	...	B. Treasures	32
2:21-24	...	B. Cameos	75
2:36-46	...	B. Cameos	42
10:13	...	B. Pinnacles	58
10:19	...	B. Treasures	109
17:7	...	B. Cameos	47
18:5-16	...	B. Treasures	33
18:39	...	B. Pinnacles	49
19:1-9	...	B. Pinnacles	49
21:3	...	B. Cameos	51
22:40-49	...	B. Pinnacles	60
2 KINGS:			
1:9-13	...	B. Cameos	53
2:11	...	B. Pinnacles	50
2:13-14	...	B. Cameos	49
2:23-24	...	B. Treasures	35
4:1-7	...	B. Treasures	33
4:8-37	...	B. Cameos	57
4:19-36	...	B. Cameos	50
4:42-44	...	B. Cameos	50
5:10-14	...	B. Cameos	50
5:15	...	B. Pinnacles	51
5:18	...	B. Pinnacles	51
6:5-7	...	B. Pinnacles	20
6:20	...	B. Cameos	50
7:10	...	B. Cameos	55
9:1-6	...	B. Pinnacles	53
9:30-33	...	B. Pinnacles	18
10:15	...	B. Pinnacles	53
11:1-3	...	B. Cameos	59
11:17-18	...	B. Treasures	42
12:2	...	B. Treasures	41
12:9	...	B. Cameos	59
13:20-21	...	B. Cameos	50
22:14	...	B. Pinnacles	55
25:27-30	...	B. Cameos	61

Reference		Book	Page
1 CHRONICLES:			
4:9-10	...	B. Treasures	37
10:13	...	B. Pinnacles	42
2 CHRONICLES:			
9:1-12	...	B. Pinnacles	57
14:8-12	...	B. Cameos	63
16:12	...	B. Cameos	63
18:6-8	...	B. Treasures	39
18:31	...	B. Treasures	39
20:20	...	B. Pinnacles	59
20:35-37	...	B. Pinnacles	59
21:20	...	B. Treasures	41
24:15-25	...	B. Treasures	41
26:3-21	...	B. Treasures	43
27:1-2	...	B. Treasures	43
28:24	...	B. Treasures	44
33:12-13	...	B. Cameos	65
EZRA:			
2:62	...	B. Pinnacles	61
9:6	...	B. Treasures	7
NEHEMIAH:			
3:1	...	B. Cameos	67
4:17	...	B. Cameos	68
13:6	...	B. Pinnacles	63
13:10	...	B. Pinnacles	63
13:28	...	B. Pinnacles	64
ESTHER:			
2:5-10	...	B. Pinnacles	65
4:13-14	...	B. Pinnacles	65
JOB:			
1:8	...	B. Treasures	66
1:9-10	...	B. Pinnacles	73
3:3-17	...	B. Cameos	69
14:14	...	B. Pinnacles	155
19:25	...	B. Cameos	69
23:3-5	...	B. Cameos	70
23:10	...	B. Cameos	70
40:4	...	B. Treasures	7
42:10	...	B. Cameos	70
PSALM:			
23:4	...	B. Pinnacles	67
27:4	...	B. Treasures	89
34:6-8	...	B. Pinnacles	69
34:8	...	B. Treasures	110
42:5	...	B. Pinnacles	58
51:5	...	B. Treasures	7
51:11	...	B. Cameos	12

PSALM:			PAGE
51:12	...	B. Pinnacles	112
68:13	...	B. Cameos	71
84:3	...	B. Treasures	45
90:2	...	B. Pinnacles	78
91:1	...	B. Pinnacles	78
91:1	...	B. Treasures	24
137	...	B. Cameos	73
137:1	...	B. Pinnacles	73
137:5	...	B. Treasures	18

PROVERBS:

1:10	...	B. Pinnacles	60
14:12	...	B. Cameos	64
24:30-34	...	B. Treasures	47
25:11	...	B. Pinnacles	67
30:18-19	...	B. Pinnacles	71
30:24-28	...	B. Treasures	49

ECCLESIASTES:

9:14-15	...	B. Treasures	51
10:1	...	B. Treasures	53
10:8	...	B. Pinnacles	73

SONG OF SOLOMON:

5:1-6	...	B. Cameos	75
5:10-16	...	B. Treasures	114
6:10	...	B. Treasures	55

ISAIAH:

1:66	...	B. Pinnacles	75
2:4	...	B. Pinnacles	86
6:5	...	B. Treasures	8
9:6	...	B. Cameos	139
9:6	...	B. Treasures	113
12:3	...	B. Treasures	57
30:20-26	...	B. Treasures	59
37:14	...	B. Pinnacles	77
37:21-36	...	B. Pinnacles	78
40:31	...	B. Pinnacles	5
42:13	...	B. Treasures	61
49:15	...	B. Treasures	18
52:11	...	B. Pinnacles	24
53	...	B. Treasures	63
53:9	...	B. Treasures	114
55:1	...	B. Pinnacles	20
61:10	...	B. Pinnacles	55
65:24	...	B. Pinnacles	65

JEREMIAH:

17:21-23	...	B. Pinnacles	73
18:1-6	...	B. Pinnacles	79

			PAGE
JEREMIAH:			
20:9	...	B. Pinnacles	149
31:34	...	B. Cameos	42
36:23	...	B. Cameos	77
38:7-13	...	B. Pinnacles	81
39:16-18	...	B. Pinnacles	82
EZEKIEL:			
1:28	...	B. Pinnacles	168
14:14	...	B. Treasures	65
DANIEL:			
3:25	...	B. Cameos	79
5:5-28	...	B. Cameos	74
12:2-3	...	B. Cameos	128
JONAH:			
1:1-3	...	B. Cameos	81
HAGGAI:			
1:6	...	B. Treasures	67
ZECHARIAH:			
3:1-7	...	B. Treasures	69
MATTHEW:			
1:5	...	B. Pinnacles	22
2:1-2	...	B. Cameos	83
3:16-17	...	B. Pinnacles	157
3:17	...	B. Pinnacles	83
6:25-30	...	B. Treasures	82
6:33	...	B. Treasures	68
8:1-3	...	B. Cameos	50
8:4	...	B. Pinnacles	141
8:13	...	B. Pinnacles	102
8:28	...	B. Cameos	85
10:34	...	B. Pinnacles	85
11:21-23	...	B. Cameos	101
11:28	...	B. Treasures	71
11:28	...	B. Treasures	72
12:14-21	...	B. Treasures	61
12:22-32	...	B. Treasures	73
12:42	...	B. Pinnacles	58
12:43-45	...	B. Cameos	87
13:44	...	B. Treasures	75
14:10	...	B. Cameos	89
14:12	...	B. Treasures	77
14:29	...	B. Pinnacles	87
15:22	...	B. Cameos	91
15:22-28	...	B. Treasures	82
15:23	...	B. Treasures	79
15:30	...	B. Cameos	93

MATTHEW: PAGE

16:9-10	B. Cameos		50
16:21	B. Pinnacles		20
16:26	B. Treasures		6
16:28	B. Treasures		153
17:5	B. Pinnacles		83
17:19-21	B. Treasures		95
17:20	B. Treasures		81
17:24	B. Pinnacles		89
17:27	B. Pinnacles		89
19:27-29	B. Pinnacles		92
19:29	B. Pinnacles		12
20:9	B. Pinnacles		91
21:12-14	B. Pinnacles		122
22:12	B. Pinnacles		93
23:37	B. Treasures		60
24:37-39	B. Cameos		3
25:1-13	B. Pinnacles		108
25:1-13	B. Treasures		83
26:12	B. Cameos		95
27:12-14	B. Treasures		80
27:32	B. Cameos		123
27:36	B. Pinnacles		117
27:42	B. Pinnacles		159
27:45-52	B. Pinnacles		95
27:46	B. Cameos		97
27:54	B. Pinnacles		117
27:57-60	B. Treasures		63
28:1	B. Cameos		147
28:20	B. Pinnacles		120

MARK:

3:14-19	B. Pinnacles		113
3:18	B. Treasures		112
3:21-31	B. Cameos		143
5:22	B. Cameos		99
6:7-12	B. Treasures		85
6:35-38	B. Treasures		110
6:41	B. Treasures		107
7:31-37	B. Pinnacles		97
8:22-26	B. Cameos		101
8:36	B. Treasures		87
9:38	B. Pinnacles		18
10:21	B. Treasures		89
10:47	B. Cameos		103
10:49-52	B. Cameos		104
14:3	B. Treasures		91
14:67	B. Cameos		121
14:68	B. Pinnacles		74

MARK:

			PAGE
14:71	...	B. Cameos	122
15:39	...	B. Cameos	146
16:2	...	B. Cameos	148
16:7	...	B. Cameos	122
16:12	...	B. Pinnacles	99
16:15	...	B. Pinnacles	120

LUKE:

1:7	...	B. Pinnacles	8
1:29-35	...	B. Pinnacles	8
1:32-33	...	B. Treasures	83
1:35	...	B. Pinnacles	132
2:11	...	B. Pinnacles	119
2:44	...	B. Cameos	105
4:1	...	B. Pinnacles	132
4:14	...	B. Pinnacles	132
4:16-22	...	B. Pinnacles	56
4:18	...	B. Pinnacles	132
5:1-11	...	B. Treasures	93
5:8	...	B. Treasures	8
5:17	...	B. Cameos	107
5:18-20	...	B. Treasures	95
6:6	...	B. Treasures	95
7:1-10	...	B. Pinnacles	101
7:1-10	...	B. Treasures	82
7:6	...	B. Treasures	8
7:15	...	B. Cameos	50
7:15	...	B. Treasures	97
7:24	...	B. Cameos	113
7:28	...	B. Treasures	87
7:37	...	B. Cameos	109
7:48	...	B. Treasures	114
8:3	...	B. Pinnacles	103
8:4-15	...	B. Treasures	99
8:37	...	B. Cameos	111
8:43-44	...	B. Pinnacles	105
8:55	...	B. Treasures	97
9:28-31	...	B. Pinnacles	157
9:32	...	B. Pinnacles	107
9:62	...	B. Pinnacles	109
10:25	...	B. Treasures	101
10:30	...	B. Pinnacles	111
10:34-35	...	B. Treasures	103
10:40	...	B. Cameos	95
10:42	...	B. Treasures	89
12:16	...	B. Cameos	115
14:14	...	B. Cameos	128
15:12	...	B. Pinnacles	112

			PAGE
LUKE:			
15:12-13	...	B. Pinnacles	73
15:15-15	...	B. Cameos	117
17:14	...	B. Pinnacles	141
17:28-32	...	B. Treasures	10
18:1	...	B. Pinnacles	163
18:18	...	B. Treasures	101
18:35-43	...	B. Cameos	50
19:3	...	B. Cameos	119
19:30	...	B. Treasures	113
19:41-44	...	B. Pinnacles	126
22:3-5	...	B. Pinnacles	113
22:19	...	B. Treasures	107
22:31-32	...	B. Treasures	105
22:39-45	...	B. Pinnacles	108
22:43	...	B. Pinnacles	116
22:44	...	B. Pinnacles	150
22:55	...	B. Cameos	121
22:62	...	B. Pinnacles	74
23:8-9	...	B. Treasures	80
23:26	...	B. Cameos	123
23:28	...	B. Cameos	124
23:33	...	B. Pinnacles	117
23:41	...	B. Cameos	127
23:42	...	B. Pinnacles	117
23:42-43	...	B. Cameos	125
23:55	...	B. Pinnacles	104
24:10	...	B. Pinnacles	104
24:30-31	...	B. Treasures	108
24:35	...	B. Treasures	107
JOHN:			
1:14	...	B. Pinnacles	119
1:29	...	B. Cameos	167
1:39	...	B. Treasures	109
1:40-42	...	B. Treasures	111
1:51	...	B. Pinnacles	14
2:5	...	B. Cameos	143
2:9	...	B. Cameos	129
2:13-16	...	B. Pinnacles	121
3:10	...	B. Cameos	131
3:14-15	...	B. Pinnacles	20
3:16	...	B. Cameos	50
4:1-3	...	B. Treasures	80
4:14	...	B. Cameos	133
4:52	...	B. Cameos	135
5:6	...	B. Pinnacles	123
5:24	...	B. Treasures	154
6:5-9	...	B. Treasures	112

176

JOHN: PAGE

7:46	B. Treasures	113
7:50	B. Cameos	131
7:50-52	B. Treasures	124
8:6	B. Cameos	137
8:6	B. Treasures	79
8:18	B. Pinnacles	95
8:28-29	B. Pinnacles	95
8:31	B. Treasures	113
8:52	B. Treasures	154
8:56	B. Treasures	113
9:20-21	B. Treasures	96
9:25	B. Treasures	89
9:35-38	B. Cameos	139
10:10	B. Treasures	115
10:28	B. Treasures	117
11:12	B. Pinnacles	158
11:20	B. Cameos	141
11:35	B. Pinnacles	125
11:40	B. Pinnacles	159
11:44	B. Treasures	97
12:3	B. Cameos	96
12:3	B. Treasures	54
12:4-6	B. Pinnacles	113
12:20-22	B. Treasures	113
12:24	B. Treasures	112
12:28	B. Pinnacles	84
12:42-43	B. Treasures	124
13:8	B. Pinnacles	127
13:23	B. Pinnacles	129
14:27	B. Treasures	119
15:1-5	B. Pinnacles	131
15:6	B. Pinnacles	132
15:7-8	B. Pinnacles	162
15:11	B. Pinnacles	133
15:11	B. Treasures	119
16:7	B. Pinnacles	120
16:13-15	B. Pinnacles	11
16:23-24	B. Pinnacles	133
17:5	B. Treasures	143
17:12	B. Pinnacles	114
17:13-14	B. Pinnacles	134
18:4-8	B. Treasures	121
19	B. Cameos	145
19:2	B. Pinnacles	135
19:25	B. Cameos	143
19:25-27	B. Pinnacles	118
19:26-27	B. Pinnacles	129
19:38-42	B. Treasures	123

177

JOHN:

						PAGE
19:41	...	B. Treasures	...	...	...	113
20:1	...	B. Cameos	...	...	...	147
20:17	...	B. Pinnacles	...	...	...	137
21:7	...	B. Pinnacles	...	...	...	130
21:21-22	...	B. Treasures	...	...	...	125

ACTS OF THE APOSTLES:

1:9-11	...	B. Pinnacles	...	...	...	158
1:10-11	...	B. Treasures	...	...	...	83
1:25	...	B. Pinnacles	...	...	...	114
2:39	...	B. Cameos	...	...	...	11
3:1-8	...	B. Pinnacles	...	...	...	142
3:2	...	B. Pinnacles	...	...	...	139
4:12	...	B. Pinnacles	...	...	...	128
5:38-39	...	B. Cameos	...	...	...	149
6:2-5	...	B. Cameos	...	...	...	151
6:7	...	B. Pinnacles	...	...	...	141
7:2	...	B. Cameos	...	...	...	5
8:9-10	...	B. Cameos	...	...	...	153
8:18-19	...	B. Pinnacles	...	...	...	164
8:21	...	B. Cameos	...	...	...	153
9:18-20	...	B. Cameos	...	...	...	155
9:36	...	B. Treasures	...	...	...	140
10:2	...	B. Pinnacles	...	...	...	143
10:44-48	...	B. Pinnacles	...	...	...	143
12:11	...	B. Cameos	...	...	...	118
12:12	...	B. Cameos	...	...	...	157
13:1	...	B. Pinnacles	...	...	...	145
13:13	...	B. Cameos	...	...	...	157
15:1-6	...	B. Treasures	...	...	...	127
15:37-39	...	B. Cameos	...	...	...	158
15:37-40	...	B. Treasures	...	...	...	129
16:6-8	...	B. Cameos	...	...	...	159
16:10	...	B. Cameos	...	...	...	160
17:16-34	...	B. Treasures	...	...	...	131
18:6-8	...	B. Pinnacles	...	...	..	147
18:17	...	B. Pinnacles	...	...	..	147
18:25	...	B. Pinnacles	...	...	...	149
20:7	...	B. Treasures	...	...	..	128
21:4-13	...	B. Treasures	...	...	...	133
21:8-9	...	B. Treasures	...	...	...	139
22:17-21	...	B. Treasures	...	...	...	133
24:25-27	...	B. Cameos	...	...	...	161
25:23-24	...	B. Pinnacles	...	...	...	151
26:28	...	B. Pinnacles	...	...	...	151
27:12	...	B. Pinnacles	...	...	...	153
27:13	...	B. Treasures	...	...	...	135
28:1	...	B. Treasures	...	...	...	135

ROMANS:			PAGE
5:1	...	B. Pinnacles	161
5:1	...	B. Treasures	137
5:10	...	B. Treasures	137
5:17	...	B. Treasures	115
5:19	...	B. Treasures	88
6:3-7	...	B. Treasures	20
7:24-25	...	B. Cameos	62
8:28	...	B. Treasures	136
8:32	...	B. Cameos	82
10:9	...	B. Cameos	80
11:15	...	B. Pinnacles	93
1 CORINTHIANS:			
1:1	...	B. Pinnacles	148
1:26-27	...	B. Pinnacles	103
2:1-2	...	B. Treasures	132
2:14	...	B. Pinnacles	71
3:13-15	...	B. Cameos	128
3:16	...	B. Pinnacles	122
5:1-5	...	B. Treasures	118
9:27	...	B. Pinnacles	132
13:13	...	B. Cameos	143
13:16	...	B. Pinnacles	64
14:34-35	...	B. Treasures	139
15:5	...	B. Cameos	122
15:14	...	B. Pinnacles	155
15:55	...	B. Cameos	126
2 CORINTHIANS:			
4:7	...	B. Pinnacles	28
6:14	...	B. Pinnacles	59
8:2	...	B. Treasures	115
8:9	...	B. Treasures	143
11:23-27	...	B. Cameos	163
11:24-25	...	B. Pinnacles	160
13:1	...	B. Pinnacles	157
GALATIANS:			
5:22-23	...	B. Pinnacles	162
6:1	...	B. Treasures	129
6:7-8	...	B. Pinnacles	26
EPHESIANS:			
2:1-4	...	B. Pinnacles	38
2:4-7	...	B. Treasures	70
2:6	...	B. Treasures	20
2:12-13	...	B. Treasures	145
4:1	...	B. Treasures	141
4:6	...	B. Treasures	141
4:14-15	...	B. Treasures	115

			PAGE
EPHESIANS:			
4:17	...	B. Treasures	141
5:1-2	...	B. Treasures	142
5:8	...	B. Treasures	142
5:15	...	B. Treasures	142
5:19	...	B. Treasures	55
6:11-12	...	B. Treasures	20
6:11-17	...	B. Treasures	142
PHILIPPIANS:			
1:23	...	B. Cameos	164
2:5-13	...	B. Treasures	143
3:8	...	B. Cameos	23
3:13	...	B. Treasures	89
4:13	...	B. Pinnacles	88
4:19	...	B. Cameos	62
COLOSSIANS:			
1:20	...	B. Treasures	145
2:15	...	B. Pinnacles	116
3:11	...	B. Cameos	133
4:14	...	B. Cameos	159
1 THESSALONIANS:			
1:9-10	...	B. Treasures	147
2:14-19	...	B. Treasures	147
3:12-13	...	B. Treasures	148
4:13-18	...	B. Treasures	148
4:16-18	...	B. Treasures	83
5:23	...	B. Treasures	148
2 THESSALONIANS:			
2:3	...	B. Pinnacles	114
1 TIMOTHY:			
1:1-15	...	B. Pinnacles	119
1:1-15	...	B. Treasures	8
2:11-12	...	B. Treasures	139
3:16	...	B. Pinnacles	119
2 TIMOTHY:			
1:12	...	B. Pinnacles	160
1:16-18	...	B. Treasures	149
4:6-7	...	B. Cameos	163
4:8	...	B. Pinnacles	160
4:10	...	B. Cameos	114
4:11	...	B. Cameos	160
4:19	...	B. Treasures	150
EPISTLE TO PHILEMON:			
		B. Treasures	151
HEBREWS:			
1:7-8	...	B. Treasures	143

Hebrews:				**Page**
1:14	...	B. Pinnacles	... ...	14
2:3	...	B. Cameos	... ...	62
2:9	...	B. Pinnacles	... ...	135
2:9	...	B. Treasures	... ...	153
4:11	...	B. Treasures	... ...	155
4:14	...	B. Treasures	... ...	155
4:15	...	B. Pinnacles	... ...	115
4:16	...	B. Treasures	... ...	78
4:16	...	B. Treasures	... ...	115
5:7	...	B. Pinnacles	... ...	115
5:7	...	B. Pinnacles	... ...	126
6:1	...	B. Treasures	... ...	156
6:10	...	B. Treasures	... ...	34
7:25	...	B. Pinnacles	... ...	159
9:14	...	B. Pinnacles	... ...	132
10:19-20	...	B. Treasures	... ...	146
10:24	...	B. Treasures	... ...	156
11:1	...	B. Pinnacles	... ...	159
11:5	...	B. Pinnacles	... ...	6
11:29-31	...	B. Treasures	... ...	157
12:1	...	B. Cameos	... ...	164
12:1	...	B. Treasures	... ...	32
12:2	...	B. Pinnacles	... ...	115
12:2	...	B. Treasures	... ...	120
12:16-17	...	B. Cameos	... ...	12
12:28	...	B. Treasures	... ...	156
13:8	...	B. Treasures	... ...	78
13:13	...	B. Treasures	... ...	156
13:15	...	B. Treasures	... ...	156
James:				
1:5	...	B. Pinnacles	... ...	163
4:2	...	B. Pinnacles	... ...	163
4:3	...	B. Pinnacles	... ...	164
5:14-15	...	B. Pinnacles	... ...	164
1 Peter:				
1:7-8	...	B. Pinnacles	... ...	12
1:19	...	B. Cameos	... ...	165
2:6-7	...	B. Cameos	... ...	165
2:7	...	B. Cameos	... ...	122
5:5	...	B. Pinnacles	... ...	56
2 Peter:				
1:2	...	B. Pinnacles	... ...	161
1:3	...	B. Pinnacles	... ...	162
1:8	...	B. Pinnacles	... ...	162
1:11	...	B. Treasures	... ...	115
1:14	...	B. Cameos	... ...	166
1:18	...	B. Pinnacles	... ...	107

		PAGE
2 PETER:		
2:20	... B. Pinnacles	161
3:18	... B. Pinnacles	162
1 JOHN:		
1:3-7	... B. Pinnacles	134
1:7	... B. Treasures	146
3:2	... B. Pinnacles	80
3:2	... B. Treasures	83
4:20	... B. Treasures	142
2 JOHN:		
v. 12	... B. Pinnacles	134
3 JOHN:		
	... B. Treasures	159
JUDE:		
v. 9	... B. Cameos	19
v. 14	... B. Treasures	4
vv. 14-15	... B. Pinnacles	6
REVELATION:		
1:10	... B. Treasures	60
2:2-4	... B. Pinnacles	111
2:17	... B. Treasures	161
3:7-11	... B. Pinnacles	112
3:14-22	... B. Pinnacles	165
3:20	... B. Cameos	56
4:3	... B. Pinnacles	167
5:9	... B. Cameos	4
5:9	... B. Pinnacles	118
5:9-10	... B. Treasures	70
5:9-12	... B. Treasures	146
7:14	... B. Cameos	167
7:14	... B. Treasures	163
10:1-10	... B. Pinnacles	168
12:10-12	... B. Treasures	146
19:6	... B. Treasures	144
19:12	... B. Pinnacles	135
20:11-15	... B. Pinnacles	62
20:13-14	... B. Treasures	153
21:27	... B. Treasures	163
22:1	... B. Cameos	10
22:17	... B. Treasures	163
22:20	... B. Pinnacles	158